The Getaway Guide III

Short Vacations in Northern California

by Marni and Jake Rankin

Pacific Search Press

Pacific Search Press, 222 Dexter Avenue North,
    Seattle, Washington 98109
© 1981 by Marni and Jake Rankin. All rights reserved
Printed in the United States of America

Designed by Judy Petry

All photographs by the authors except those by the following:
    Barifot, page 199
    Jim Deis, page 239
    Northstar-at-Tahoe, pages 203, 205, 206

Cover: *Corral at Greenhorn Creek Guest Ranch*

Library of Congress Cataloging in Publication Data

Rankin, Marni.
    The getaway guide III.

    1. Hotels, taverns, etc.—California—Directories.
2. Resorts—California—Directories. 3. California
—Description and travel—1951- —Guidebooks.
I. Rankin, Jake. II. Title. III. Title: Getaway
guide three. IV. Title: Short vacations in northern California.
TX907.R324   647'.94794   81-11228
ISBN 0-914718-63-0   AACR2

Wherever you go and whatever you do in the outdoors, move at Nature's pace, seeking not to impose yourself but to lose yourself. If you must leave footprints, make them not with blindness but with care and awareness of the delicate balance around you. And if you must take souvenirs, take them not in your pockets but in your mind and spirit. In preservation lies the promise of renewal.

Pacific Search Press

Contents

The Northern California Getaway. 7
The North and the North Coast 10
    Benbow Inn 11
    Flying "AA" Ranch 17
    Heritage House 24
    Konocti Harbor Inn 30
    Sea Ranch 37
    Northwood Lodge 43
    Chanslor Ranch 50
    Bodega Bay Lodge 56
    Wayside Inns
        Hartsook Inn 62
        Cobweb Palace 63
        Mendocino Hotel 64
        Joshua Grindle Inn 65
        MacCallum House Inn 66
        Glendeven 67
        Little River Inn 68
        Victorian Farmhouse 69
        Harbor House 70
        Timber Cove Inn 71
        Village Inn 72
The Wine Country 73
    Meadowood 74
    Silverado Country Club and Resort 80
    Sonoma Mission Inn 87
    Wayside Inns
        Calistoga Inn 93
        Wine Country Inn 94
        Harvest Inn 95
        Chalet Bernensis 96
        Webber Place 97
        Magnolia Hotel 98
        Burgundy House 99
        Sonoma Hotel 100

The Houseboats 101
Monterey Peninsula, Carmel Valley, and the Big Sur. 109
   Pajaro Dunes 110
   The Lodge at Pebble Beach 117
   Quail Lodge 124
   Carmel Valley Inn 131
   Ventana 137
   Wayside Inns
      Pine Inn 144
      Normandy Inn 145
      Stonehouse Guest Lodge 146
      San Antonio House 147
      Highlands Inn 148
      The Valley Lodge 149
The Gold Country 150
   Wayside Inns
      Jamestown Hotel 164
      The Gunn House 165
      City Hotel 166
      Murphys Hotel 167
      Hotel Leger 168
      Sutter Creek Inn 169
      The Mine House Inn 170
      Vineyard House 171
      National Hotel 172
      Red Castle Inn 173
The Lake Tahoe Area 174
   Greenhorn Creek Guest Ranch 175
   Royal Gorge Nordic Ski Resort 182
   Squaw Valley Lodge 189
   River Ranch 196
   Northstar-at-Tahoe 202
   Cal-Neva Lodge 209
   Tahoe's West Shore Condos 215
   Lakeland Village Beach and Ski Resort 223
   Strawberry Lodge 229
   Bear Valley Village 235
   Wayside Inn
      Mayfield House 242
Yosemite Valley 243
Checklist 254

The Northern California Getaway

To most of us, a "getaway" is quite different from a vacation. We tend to think of a vacation as a rare, formal, once-a-year event, usually involving long-distance travel, with much planning and preparation. A getaway, on the other hand, is of short duration and spur of the moment, taken when opportunity affords, usually to some place close at hand.

The Getaway Guide series was a result of our discovery that we enjoyed short getaways more than long vacations, especially because we could do them more frequently, and the benefits from a number of quick escapes spaced throughout the year were always far greater than from the same number of days taken off all at once.

But to be able to take a quick trip without much planning means you must have at least a mental list of places you want to go, including how each one might suit your current mood, what there will be to do when you arrive, what equipment you will need, and what the costs will be.

Of course, these are exactly the questions that arise when a spouse, family member, or friend says, "It looks like we could have a couple of days free next week, so why don't we just take off?" Too often the reply is, "Fine, but where will we go?" And then, as an afterthought, "Well, someone told me about a great place over east or somewhere where there is tennis and a nice restaurant, but I forget the name and it sounded a little expensive..." The project could die right there.

If the problem of deciding where to go sounds familiar, you will understand why we wrote these guides. We had started building a checklist of good places in order not to be caught without ideas again, and as it continued to grow, we decided to make it into a book. The first *Getaway Guide* listed most of the better-known places in the Pacific Northwest. The second volume was just a natural expansion of the first one, zeroing in on a group of less well-known Northwest destinations that fell more into the category of "discoveries" or hideaways.

These first books were well received by the book-buying public and because the exploration and the research is agreeable work, we decided to expand the effort into California, where many Northwesterners like to go, and which, of course, has its own, much larger population of travel-oriented people.

In undertaking this third book, we were lucky to have spent much time in California and to know permanent residents in the northern part of the state, who have many contacts and up-to-date knowledge of immense value.

For most people, anything over four hours away is far enough to go on a getaway. So it was decided to divide California in half, with Big Sur as the dividing line. This book would cover all of the getaways in northern California, using San Francisco as the base point for measuring travel distances. Southern California then would become the subject of *The Getaway Guide IV,* our next project, which will list all the places within "getaway" distance from the southern population centers.

A word of explanation is in order about how we find and decide which places to include in these books. First, we never attempt to rate or compare places with each other, or assign stars or numerical grades. To be good, places have to have individuality, so comparisons are too subjective to be useful. We try, by extensive reading and correspondence, and by talking to travel-wise people, to discover which are the best, most respected, and enjoyable places to go. Particular credence is given to inn-keepers themselves, the professionals of the business; we ask them where *they* like to go when they take time off.

After we finally have assembled a list of the most likely places, we visit them, usually spending a night or several nights to get the full flavor, participating in the activities, and sampling the food and hospitality. Then we ask ourselves, "Is this a place *we* would like to come back to, just for a good time, when we're not at work?" A solid "yes" means we write the story and put it in the book.

Northern California differs from the Northwest because of the remarkable way in which its resort and vacation areas fall neatly into about half a dozen well-defined geographical areas, each different from the others. This made it easy to divide the book into segments: the north and the north coast; the wine country; the Delta and Lake Shasta (for houseboating); Monterey Peninsula, Carmel Valley, and Big Sur; the gold country; the Lake Tahoe area; and Yosemite Valley.

Just as they differ geographically, so do they offer different kinds of accommodations. In some areas full-sized conventional resorts are the rule, in others the best places to stay are the little wayside inns, and in still others there is a choice between the two. The section on the gold country, for instance, refers only to the little inns for accommodation, because there are no regular resorts in that whole area. The north coast, however, has a number of full destination resorts, but if these are booked up or seem too formal or you just want a place to put up for the night while "doing" the country, one page is devoted to each of the many delightful wayside inns available for alternative lodgings.

The Monterey Peninsula and the wine country both offer a mix of resorts and little inns, but in the eastern part of the state, with its great cluster of resorts around Lake Tahoe, just one wayside inn sits in lonely splendor on a side street.

Everything changes with time in the resort and vacation business; places improve, places go downhill, and new ones always are being built. For these reasons, a book such as this must be revised and updated from time to time, and we appreciate nothing more than hearing from our readers with information about getaways you have especially enjoyed (including the features that made them particularly outstanding), along with anything else about resorts and inns, new or old, that would improve the contents of the next edition.

The North and the North Coast

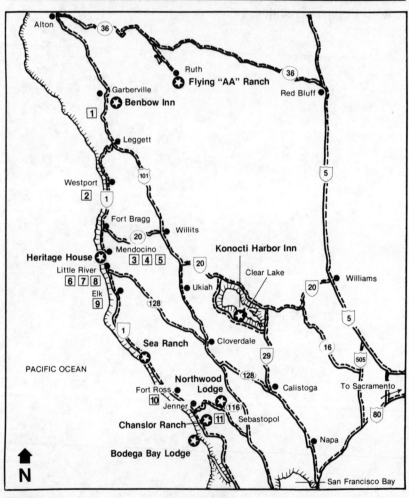

Alton · Ruth · Flying "AA" Ranch · Red Bluff · Garberville · Benbow Inn · Leggett · Westport · Fort Bragg · Willits · Konocti Harbor Inn · Heritage House · Mendocino · Clear Lake · Williams · Little River · Ukiah · Elk · Sea Ranch · Cloverdale · Fort Ross · Northwood Lodge · Calistoga · To Sacramento · Jenner · Chanslor Ranch · Sebastopol · Napa · Bodega Bay Lodge · San Francisco Bay · PACIFIC OCEAN

N

Wayside Inns

1 Hartsook Inn
2 Cobweb Palace
3 Mendocino Hotel
4 Joshua Grindle Inn
5 MacCallum House Inn
6 Glendeven

7 Little River Inn
8 Victorian Farmhouse
9 Harbor House
10 Timber Cove Inn
11 Village Inn

Benbow Inn

Distances:
>   From San Francisco—200 miles; allow 4 hours
>   From Eureka—78 miles; allow 1½ hours

Features:
>   A stately castle of an inn between Benbow Lake and the Eel River, at
>   the head of California's redwood country; lavish outdoor
>   setting, with gardens, terraces, lawns, and oak trees; the inside is
>   full of antiques and Old World charm

Activities:
>   Golf, lake swimming, bicycling, par course jogging, hiking, fishing,
>   sight-seeing

Seasons:
>   From the last Friday in March until the first Monday after Thanks-
>   giving, and briefly during the year-end holidays

Rates:
>   For two people—regular rooms $44 to $64, terrace rooms $44 to $55,
>   patio suites $75, and treetop suites $80 to $100

Address:
>   2675 Benbow Drive, Garberville, California 95440

Phone:
>   (707) 923-2124

Benbow Inn is easily seen from highway

Just four hours out of San Francisco, the Benbow Inn is a favorite first-night stopping point for travelers heading north to Portland and beyond. The convenient location is one reason for its popularity, but more important is the discovery that a day spent here is a mini-vacation in itself.

To make the most out of a necessary trip north, convert the long drive into a delightful, scenic vacation. Do this by starting from the Bay Area early in order to arrive at Benbow in time for lunch on the terrace. Once there, you will be transported into a different, restful world, full of flowers and color and giant sheltering trees. Read a book, stroll about the grounds, swim in the clear lake at your doorstep, and then prepare for a long cocktail hour at dusk, on the terrace again, followed by a leisurely, elegant dinner. The next morning play an early round of golf on the course next door, and resume the drive. You actually will have spent less than twenty-four hours at the inn, but it will have seemed like a week.

Now in its fifty-fourth year, the Benbow Inn has long been a well-loved California landmark, which unfortunately changed hands too frequently and began to suffer from lack of continuity and direction. Two years ago, however, it was acquired by a friendly, ambitious couple who love the place and are filled with plans for its future.

The results of Chuck and Patsy Watts's extraordinary efforts are apparent in every phase of the operation. The extensive formal gardens have been restored, the plumbing and heating modernized, the rooms redecorated, the kitchen and dining room particularly lavished with attention, and new furniture acquired. "New" furniture may be a misuse of words; newly acquired antiques would be more accurate. The inn's lobby alone is reason enough for an antique buff to visit here. The Watts are expert collectors, and it is worth an hour or two to examine the carefully coordinated items they have assembled in this comfortable and much used room.

Beside the antiques, it is impossible to overlook another item that at first may seem to be nothing more than an unusual, large, woolly throw rug. But throw rugs don't breathe, and this one will turn out to be Muffin, the Watts's affable Afghan hound, who likes to arrange herself in some cool spot in the lobby, and has become the trademark of the new Benbow.

Routes and Distances

The Benbow Inn is prominently visible just west of Highway 101, two miles south of Garberville. The Benbow exit is clearly marked, with the green fairways of the golf course in the background. Take the exit and follow the signs to the inn.

Accommodations

Old-timers who knew the inn in earlier days can only be thrilled with the refurbishments and renovations, which have been done without losing any of the resort's old grandeur. The basic structure, with over sixty rooms, is the same except that a broad carpeted stairway—with heavy, polished balustrades and antiques furnishing the landings—now leads from the lobby to the rooms on the floors above.

Not only is the building tall, with three floors of rooms above the main level, but it also is built on a hillside, which allows two additional levels of accommodations below, providing a broad assortment of choices.

Most numerous are the rooms on the second and third levels. All of these open off wide cherry-wainscoted hallways, each with an old-fashioned smoked-glass transom embellished with the room number above the door. Inside, the rooms have high ceilings and lots of light (many have a big bay window) and lovely views of the lake or the formal gardens and the terrace. Their furnishings are antiques or fine reproductions, with chintz bedspreads and matching drapes that add to the old-time atmosphere. All of these rooms have private baths and showers, with rates varying slightly due to room size and outlook.

On the lofty heights of the uppermost floor are eight newly installed deluxe suites, referred to as the treetop units. They are extra large and prettily furnished, with individual wood-burning fireplaces and expansive views.

Two other kinds of units on the lower levels are quite different. These have private entrances opening either to the lawn or onto a long, latticed

Sunny front entrance of Benbow Inn

terrace. On the lawn level are four garden units facing a flower-framed patio. Like the treetop units, these are suites with bedrooms, baths, and sitting rooms, with patio furniture outside. Just above them are the terrace rooms, each of which also has its own outdoor furniture and consists of a big bedroom with a sitting area and a bath. Both the garden and terrace rooms are furnished in white wicker with white iron bedsteads and colorful spreads for a cheerful effect.

Activities

Originally, this whole section of the Eel River Valley, nearly three thousand acres, was owned by the Benbow family, a large clan that conceived and executed the gigantic task of building the original hotel, a great part of it by their own labor. That was in 1926. Since then the property has been broken up, but not before Benbow Lake was created by the damming of the Eel and the golf course was laid out in the rolling hills to the east.

The crescent-shaped lake comes right up to the lawn behind the inn, forming a lovely vista flanked on both sides by English gardens and shaded by giant oaks. At the water's edge, a little sandy beach provides a favorite place for guests to swim. To the front of the inn are more gardens, and beyond them a public park borders on the other end of the curved lake. There are barbecues and picnic tables in the park, with a large playground for children and a par-course jogging track that zigzags along the water's edge and through clumps of trees and meadows.

Although the Benbow Valley Golf Course is no longer owned by the inn itself, it is now a public course, available to inn guests. Under the highway, there is even a special tunnel that connects the two properties, making the pro shop and first tee only a short walk away. The course is well maintained and has some challenging holes. Greens fees are moderate, and bicycles also can be rented, by the hour or by the day, at the pro shop.

For those who like to roam on foot, there are interesting trails in the hills behind the inn and along the river above the dam. The management will provide wicker-basket picnics for hikers, as well as suggestions about sunny meadow sites or riverside destinations. At certain times of the year, when the water level is high, the Eel can be a fair trout producer. Fishermen might like to take a rod and flies on their hikes.

For a different type of picnic, you can take your basket lunch for a day on the "squirrel bus," which picks up guests every morning at ten for all-day tours of the surrounding area. This open-topped vehicle drives through the most impressive of the nearby redwood groves, then visits a large redwood sawmill and the restored Victorian village of Ferndale before returning to the inn in time for cocktails.

With all these choices of outings, there nevertheless are quite a number of guests who seem content to sit in a quiet alcove with a book from the inn's big library or just relax out on the lawn or terrace, perhaps with something cool from the bar.

In the evening, or on occasional days when the weather is inclement, there is always a fire in the lobby's fireplace, and bridge, gin rummy, and chess games are popular ways to pass the time. A piano player in the bar in the evenings plays old favorites on request, and every night after dinner one of the Benbow Inn's most popular traditions is the free showing of a classic old-time movie, to which all guests are invited.

Dining

Be sure to make dinner reservations as soon as you check in at the Benbow Inn. There are no comparable restaurants in the area, so people come from all around and the dining room is often crowded. During summer months dinner, as well as lunch and the popular Sunday champagne brunch, is served on the terrace and in the dining room.

The large, elegant dining room is done in Tudor decor. A magnificent hand-carved antique buffet graces one wall, with other heavy dark pieces scattered here and there. The tables are set with white linen, fresh flowers, and pewter serving plates.

The entrées comprise a well-balanced list of meat and seafood items, including an outstanding veal piccata and a fine New York pepper steak done in a robust, mushroom-filled sauce. Fish lovers are offered a catch-

Luncheon and cocktails are served on Benbow Inn terrace

of-the-day, as well as a good selection of standard items. The wine list is especially fun because it has been chosen entirely from smaller, little-known family wineries throughout northern California. It provides an unusual opportunity to sample many of these more obscure, but often excellent, vintages.

Flying "AA" Ranch

Distances:

From San Francisco—323 miles; allow 8 hours by automobile, 1½ hours by airplane

From Eureka—100 miles; allow 2½ hours

Features:

A combination resort–guest ranch deep within Trinity County's Mad River valley, one of northern California's more remote, pristine forest areas; particularly popular as a fly-in destination for private pilots

Activities:

Horseback riding, hiking, bicycling, tennis, trapshooting, fishing, hunting, hayrides, barbecues, dancing, and pool, lake, and river swimming

Seasons:

Mid-April through mid-December, but schedule varies slightly with the weather

Rates:

Rates for two people range from $15 for a tent-cabin to $37 for a hotel room, with meals a la carte; midweek five-day packages, including all meals plus riding and certain other amenities, $310 per person

Address:

P.O. Box 97, Ruth, California 95526

Phones:

(707) 574-6227 or (707) 574-6417

Flying "AA" ranch house and pool

The old AA Ranch was named for the original owner, an Indian lady with the unlikely name of Ann Anderson, who raised cattle and horses, but was wiped out when a devastating winter killed all of her livestock and she walked away from the property. The name stuck, however, through subsequent ownerships until Larry Brown, a pilot, purchased it and added an airstrip and the word "Flying" to the title—hence, the Flying "AA" Ranch.

And flying is an important part of the operation. Over half of the guests each summer come in by air, and it is a popular destination for mass fly-ins by aviation clubs and pilots' organizations. On some weekends it is easy to count twenty-five to thirty-five planes of all sorts and sizes on the tarmac, and flying is the prevalent topic of conversation around the pool and the bar where strangers get acquainted, swapping stories and information.

Few places in California are as remote as the Flying "AA," located deep in the mountainous Shasta-Trinity National Forest, and only a short distance from the little-known, roadless Yolla Bolly Wilderness. When we drove in for our first visit on the highway from Red Bluff, after passing the tiny town of Platina, we recorded meeting only three cars in either direction all the way to Mad River, a distance of fifty-three miles. At the ranch itself there are no newspapers, no televisions, and not even a radio (except for the CBs and shortwave sets crackling in the office, maintaining contact with planes coming in and ranch hands working in outlying areas).

The lack of news of the world and its crises is a bit unnerving to people accustomed to having these things served up every morning with breakfast and again with the evening news. But it does not take long for such lack to become a distinct pleasure. You suddenly realize out here you really *have* gotten away from it all, and you really can relax. As one first-timer remarked, "The nice thing about this place is just thinking about all the things I'm *not* going to do all day."

Other nice things are the clear air (conducive to long, restful sleep), the blue skies and sunny days, and the variety of things to do if you should nevertheless feel the inclination to be active.

The Flying "AA" is a big ranch; its owners control or lease some 17,000 acres of forest and grazing land. The guest facilities alone have three miles of traditional white board fencing enclosing the many pastures, corrals, and paddocks. The lower trunks of the pines and firs that grace the grounds are painted white, too, to match the fences, an indication of the care and concern devoted to appearances and maintenance. It is an atmosphere that carries over to the staff in the form of traditional western hospitality; employees can be counted on to greet new guests with a "hiyah!" and a genuinely pleasant and accommodating demeanor. Western dress is standard for all activities and events here, and informality prevails.

Routes and Distances

From the San Francisco Bay area the most direct route is to take U.S. 101 north for 256 miles to the little town of Alton, 22 miles short of Eureka. At Alton turn east on Route 36 for 48 miles of winding, narrow mountain roads until you get to Mad River (don't blink or you might miss it). At Mad River a side road forks off toward Ruth Lake. The town of Ruth, consisting of a general store with gas pumps, is at the south end of the lake. Flying "AA" Ranch is 5 miles south of Ruth. A nice way to make this trip is to drive four hours to Garberville and spend one night at the Benbow Inn (see the preceding chapter), then do the second half in a leisurely fashion the next day.

From Sacramento the shortest way is to follow Interstate 5 129 miles north to Red Bluff, where you pick up the same Route 36, but this time head west for 96 miles to get to Mad River. Long portions of this drive are the essence of mountain driving, with continuous hairpin turns and steep grades. The several settlements en route are tiny and far apart so be sure your car is in good shape and the gas tank filled. Driving is necessarily slow, but there is little traffic and the scenery is beautiful and fully worth the effort. Plan to allow plenty of time and take a picnic to enjoy at one of the outstanding promontories along the way.

Pilots have the best of it getting to the Flying "AA." Its three-thousand-foot paved runway (designated as RUTH, an uncontrolled airport on the maps) is a smooth asphalt strip with the tie-down area just a short walk from the ranch house. Pilots are always welcome, with no tie-down charges. Fuel is available.

Accommodations

The guest facilities at the Flying "AA" are laid out with the ranch house in the center and the various accommodations, barns, and out-buildings ranged around it. The dining room in the ranch house looks east where it gets the morning sun. Outside, above the swimming pool, is a deck with picnic tables for eating outdoors under the shade of a large oak that grows right through the floorboards. The deck narrows into a short flight of stairs, and then spreads out again in a railed circle around another very large tree with an unusual circular dovecote built around its trunk. From this central vantage point (a nice place by the way to sip a cool drink in the evening), you can watch the barns and airstrip and monitor practically everything going on at the ranch.

The type of accommodation you take should depend partly on the weather. In April and early May, and again in late fall, nights are often nippy enough in the Mad River country for temperatures to dip below freezing, and early risers on their way to breakfast sometimes will find frost still visible on roofs and railings. At those times, a room with heat is a necessity, although the temperature rises with the sun, and daytime quickly becomes pleasantly warm.

Later in the summer the valley can be hot at midday, making early mornings and late afternoons the best times for vigorous sport. Nights

Entrance to Flying "AA" Ranch

Flying "AA" "bunkhouse" and barbecue pit

even then are usually cool enough for a blanket, but not cold. That is when the tent-cabins are popular. There are ten of these modestly priced units. Each one is set on its own wooden deck surrounded by a railing and simply furnished inside with two wide bunks and bedding, a nightstand with a lamp, two chairs, and a supply of towels. Men's and women's baths, each with a stall shower, are nearby. With outdoor living the general rule, no one is inclined to spend more time than necessary indoors, and these little dwellings are quite sufficient, fitting many people to a tee. In any event, they are an unusual innovation for a resort, and are always filled at the height of the season.

The ranch's mainstay accommodations, nevertheless, are its twenty-four regular hotel-type rooms, furnished comfortably, and including queen- or king-sized beds and private baths. These are located in two main buildings, and there are an additional four smaller units in a third, movable building close by. An assortment of six other miscellaneous cottages, houses, and trailer-quarters scattered on the property and available for rent to larger groups and families completes the array of accommodation choices. All told, the Flying "AA" can put up 125 guests when every unit is filled to capacity.

Capacity or not, it is sometimes difficult to turn away members of the flying fraternity when it is so easy to pop over to the ranch in a light plane from any place in northern California. In fact, on summer weekends there have been times when guests have been known to take a chance and then, unable to get a room, have rolled out a sleeping bag under the shelter of a wing—not a preferred practice to be sure, but one that illustrates the popularity of the ranch and the clemency of its weather.

Activities

For a place in the heart of nowhere there is a surprising variety of things to do at the Flying "AA." All the activities normally associated with a guest ranch are available, as well as many other features not ordinarily expected so far from civilization. Most notable are two regulation, black asphalt tennis courts and a heated swimming pool. Still another is the rack of rental ten-speed bicycles, which are especially fun because of the beautiful scenery in the Mad River valley and the essentially level roadways with virtually no automobile traffic.

Of course, at a guest ranch the traditional way to see the countryside is on horseback, and the Flying "AA" maintains a string of twenty-four saddle animals, with a professional wrangler to lead rides. Rivers, meadows, and mountain trails provide a diversified terrain for ranch guests to explore. Hikers, of course, can use all the same trails for walking.

Besides riding, the Mad River and seven-mile-long Ruth Lake, formed when the river was dammed, attract fishermen. Trout, bass, catfish, perch, and even steelhead are taken from these waters, with possibly the best catches coming from the portion of the river just below the dam. Charter boat rentals are available at a marina on Ruth Lake, located about four-teen miles from the ranch.

In late fall, hunting becomes the focal point and the ranch is head-quarters for sportsmen who fan out over hundreds of miles of surrounding territory. Hunting is not allowed on the ranch itself, except by special invitation, but the national forest land all around, and particularly the Yolla Bolly Wilderness, abound with small black-tailed deer and black bear, with quail and doves in the meadowlands.

For practice, the ranch has a first-class five-station automatic trap-shooting range on the premises. Guests can bring their own guns and shells, or rent whatever they need, and on any weekend afternoon there is always a crowd of shooters brushing up their skills at this popular sport.

In the evenings guests play volleyball or pitch horseshoes on the lawn below the pool, while others gather in the bar or on the deck for beverages. Occasionally, there is impromptu entertainment in the bar, and on one or two nights a week dances are held, which are considered a lot of fun and attract ranch guests as well as local residents from up and down the valley.

Dining

Every day during the long guest season, three ranch-style meals are served in the big, informal dining room at the ranch. Ask the cook what time meals are and she will tell you that you can be taken care of just about any time you show up—one good example of the kind of hospitality and friendliness you can expect at the Flying "AA."

Much of the fun of getting acquainted with other guests takes place before dinner in the long western-style bar adjoining the dining room. Later, guests who discover common interests enjoy pairing up at the same table for dinner. Initially, conversations are apt to center around the hunting lodge atmosphere of the ranch house, where bear skins are stretched out on the rough wood-plank walls and numerous deer heads and game birds are mounted around the room. One of the most interesting trophies is a sleek stuffed bobcat standing on a counter where he surveys the crowd with cunning feline eyes.

For weekend dudes all the meals are served a la carte. The same is true for midweek visitors who just stay a couple of days, but for those arriving on Sunday noon to spend five days, an attractive package plan lumps all meals, as well as seven hours of horseback riding and three hours of bicycle use, under a single rate.

The Flying "AA" has a well-deserved reputation for serving excellent food in hearty ranch-size portions. You are well advised to work and play hard to keep even on the scales. Breakfasts are typical farm fare, with thickly sliced bacon, eggs, hashbrowns, and all the flapjacks you can eat. For lunch and dinner the specialties are barbecued dishes and a variety of cuts of steak.

But Saturday night is the big night for dining at the ranch. It is then that the owner, Larry Brown, fires up the outdoor barbecue and puts on a feast that attracts members of the local population as far as seventy miles away. But when the coals get going in the huge three- by nine-foot pit they will cook enough spareribs and chicken to take care of any sized crowd. On barbecue night everyone enjoys eating outside at one of the many picnic tables set out on the deck and lawn in front of the lodge. Larry presides over the whole operation himself, and after he has surfeited his guests with the good cooking, he caps it off by taking anyone who wants to go on a jolly moonlight hayride.

Heritage House

Distances:

From San Francisco—143 miles; allow 3½ hours

From Eureka—154 miles; allow 3½ hours

Features:

A big resort that carefully and elegantly mixes old-style traditions with modern services and facilities; accommodations in spacious cottages with stunning views of the Pacific; excellent meals served in a farmhouse that dates back to the 1800s; never advertised, it is nevertheless one of California's most popular resorts

Activities:

Strolling the grounds, exploring the historic town of Mendocino, tennis and golf nearby, swimming and canoeing in Big River, beachcombing, sunbathing

Seasons:

Reservations always advisable; closed December and January for maintenance

Rates:

$86 to $134 for two people; on modified American plan, which includes breakfast and dinner

Address:

Little River, California 95456

Phone:

(707) 937-5885

Main entrance of Heritage House

Heritage House is so well established and held in such high regard that it is not always easy to get reservations when you want them, but it is always worth trying. The resort is located on twenty-five acres along a rugged coastline that is notorious for its crashing surf. The original building, a farmhouse that is now used for the reception area and dining room, was built in 1877 by the present owner's grandfather. It was constructed in an architectural style strongly influenced by the New Englanders who originally settled the Mendocino area. They came to harvest the great redwoods that abounded inland, cutting the trees along Big River, then floating the logs down to sawmills in Mendocino at the river's mouth. In its heyday, Mendocino was one of the coast's most thriving and boisterous towns.

In 1949, when the Dennen family returned from the East to the family homestead and saw the old Victorian farmhouse standing in such a beautiful setting by the sea, they decided to restore it and start an inn. Since then, every effort has been made to reflect the flavor of the old Mendocino community. Furniture and antiques have been collected from the area over the years. Even old buildings from the environs have been brought in and reassembled on the property. For example, the cozy Apple Lounge, now appended to the original farmhouse, was once an apple storehouse on a nearby farm. Today it still has its original heavy timber beams and a walk-in fireplace, and is furnished with antiques and chintz couches. (These features, plus a magnificent ocean view, make it a wonderful place to socialize.) As Heritage House grew in reputation over the years and the few rooms in the old farmhouse could no longer meet the demand, guest cottages gradually were built, scattered randomly along the bluff to take advantage of the ocean views.

From the furnishings and appointments of the rooms to the preparation and serving of food to the maintenance of the grounds, Heritage House is characterized by meticulous attention to detail. Everything is carried off in a way that leaves nothing to be desired, making this, in the words of one loyal guest, "the hedonist's perfect hideaway." In fact, when standing near the front desk at check-out time, it is not unusual to hear patrons making reservations for their next visit a full year in advance.

Routes and Distances

From San Francisco, take U.S. 101 north eighty-eight miles to Cloverdale, then cross the coastal hills diagonally on Route 128 to its intersection with Highway 1. Drive north two miles to Albion and two miles past that look for the Heritage House sign on the left.

Coming from the north, turn west at Willits on Route 20, which goes to Fort Bragg. Go south from there on Highway 1, through Mendocino and Little River. Heritage House is about three miles south of Little River on the right.

Heritage House cottages line bluff above the sea

Accommodations

Heritage House began over thirty years ago with just three rooms for rent in the original old farmhouse. Today it has expanded to sixty units, the bulk of which are separate cottages of many sizes and styles, built at different times, but scattered harmoniously among clumps of pines along a high bluff overlooking the coastline. The eight newest units are known as the annex because they are located several lots south of the main twenty-six-acre property. Being the newest, these have some of the nicest rooms, also close to the bluff, with spectacular 180-degree views from spacious private decks.

Each of the Heritage House accommodations has a personality of its own, with hardly any two alike. Some cottages are formal with elegant furniture and fine antiques, while others are informal with hooked rugs and comfortable overstuffed furniture. Many units have fireplaces, and all are individually named so that, when making reservations, old-timers who know exactly which one they want will request, for example, The Opera House or The Watertower or Maison Four. Prices in the tariff schedule vary primarily according to the relative size and views of the different units.

Activities

Unlike many resorts, Heritage House does not provide recreational facilities for its guests, but judging by the popularity of the place, this is hardly a problem. Guests seem content to stroll the beautiful grounds along the ocean's edge, looking into the hidden coves and inlets that once were the hiding places of smugglers, or just sitting on their view decks, reading or loafing.

For the less sedentary, there are plenty of more active diversions in the neighborhood, with the little town of Mendocino, just a couple of miles away, the main attraction. The timber and the sawmills are long gone, but the town still exactly resembles a proper New England fishing village, as if it had been transplanted *in toto* from Cape Gloucester itself. All the stores and hotels on Main Street stand in a row facing the bay, with only an open field between them and the water. The architecture and individuality of the buildings are reasons enough to explore the streets and back alleys, but the town also has attracted many artists and craftsmen and has become a center for creative activities. It is easy to spend a whole afternoon just exploring the Mendocino Arts Center, two blocks off Main Street, where a performing arts theater, galleries, and studios feature actors, artists, sculptors, woodworkers, and weavers at work.

Between Mendocino and Heritage House are several other outstanding attractions. A wide sandy beach at the confluence of Big River and the ocean is a fine place for sunbathing and beachcombing. Upstream from this beach canoes can be rented for exploring the lazy waters of the river. In addition, both tennis and golf are available nearby. The most conve-

Shopping in Mendocino

nient golf course is at the Little River Inn. Rated 67.8, it is a par seventy-one course with eleven actual holes (seven of the first nine are played twice to make the full eighteen). Three miles east of Mendocino, on Little Lake Road, is the new Mendocino Tennis Club with three excellent hard-surfaced courts. Though it is a private club, nonmembers are welcome to play for a nominal fee. Reservations are advisable and can be made by calling (707) 937-0007.

Dining

Dining at Heritage House is perhaps the highlight of the day for its guests. Since the inn is on the modified American plan (breakfast and dinner are included in the rates), all of those staying here have an automatic reservation and can be seated in the dining room anytime between 6:00 and 8:00 P.M. Most enjoy having a leisurely cocktail around the Apple Lounge's fireplace before going in to dinner.

The main dining room is large and airy with a row of windows along the view side, while adjacent to it is the more intimate, sunken Garden Room, with an even more spectacular view of the ocean. Dinners are served formally in both rooms and guests are encouraged to dress accordingly: men in jackets and ties and women in dresses or pantsuits. At breakfast, however, informal attire is acceptable.

Dinner is served in four excellent courses with the diner choosing one

The beach at Mendocino

of the two different entrées served each evening and one of a variety of desserts. These are preceded by a soup of the day and a house salad. Wine can be selected from a long, impressive list of domestic and imported selections.

The reputation Heritage House has for serving fine dinners carries over to its breakfasts. Guests first help themselves to a buffet of fresh fruits and juices, then settle down at a table, complete with a toaster and a selection of homemade breads, to await eggs, sausage, bacon, hot cakes, and so on.

For lunch, guests are on their own. Most go into town to eat in the lovely solar dining room at the Mendocino Hotel, or to sit on the second-story deck overlooking Main Street at Brannon's Seaview Restaurant, or to pick up food at the store in Little River for a picnic on the beach.

Konocti Harbor Inn

Distances:

From San Francisco—128 miles; allow 2½ hours

From Sacramento—122 miles; allow 2½ hours

Features:

The largest and most versatilely equipped resort in northern California; located on the shores of the state's largest natural lake in an area renowned for its sunny weather

Activities:

Tennis, swimming, boating, waterskiing, fishing, golf, miniature golf, bicycling, hiking, rock hunting

Seasons:

Year around; June, July, and August are heavily booked; winter season from 1 November through mid-April

Rates:

Deluxe hotel rooms—$50 for two people in summer, $45 in winter; apartments—$80 for two to four people in summer, $72 in winter; beach cottages—$85 for four people in summer, $77 in winter

Address:

8727 Soda Bay Road, Kelseyville, California 95451

Phone:

(707) 279-4281 or toll free (800) 862-4930

Mount Konocti looms behind Konocti Harbor Inn

Konocti is a resort of grandiose proportions regardless of whether it is measured by its layout, setting, or history. Sprawled over a large portion of the waterfront section of a 127-acre property, this diversified vacation complex has numerous buildings housing 250 separate guest accommodations. The hub of the resort is the lodge, a rambling wooden structure perched on the western shore of the beautiful blue waters of Clear Lake.

Behind the resort looms Mount Konocti, an extinct volcano that was pushed two thousand feet into the sky by an eruption eons ago. This area is steeped in Indian lore and the mountain is the source of many superstitions. The Promo Indians, a gentle people who were the original inhabitants, thought the mountain was created by their mighty chief, Konocti, during a battle with a rival chief who was one of his daughter's suitors. For many years the Promo Indians enjoyed a bountiful existence from fishing, hunting, and gathering nuts and berries in the shadow of their mountain. Then peace was interrupted by the white man, and war and disease eventually wiped out most of the tribe.

An interim period in Clear Lake history began in the late 1800s when many mineral springs, which had been created by volcanic activity, were discovered. Spas and hotels sprang up and ladies and gentlemen came over rutty dirt roads in fine carriages to enjoy the medicinal benefits of the waters, as well as the serenity of the countryside. This tradition continued into the early 1900s when changing tastes and fires and other disasters closed down the grand hotels.

It was not until the building of Konocti Harbor Inn in 1960 that a whole new era began in the lovely Clear Lake region. While taking great care in constructing the resort to preserve the natural beauty of the area, the developers also took advantage of the many recreational possibilities, including swimming, fishing, boating, waterskiing, tennis, golf, hiking, and bicycling.

Despite all these features, it is still the sheer natural beauty of the Clear Lake country that is the major attraction of the resort. The mild weather and the fertile soil created by volcanic ash combine to make Lake County ideal for growing grapes, pears, and walnuts. It is always a pleasure to drive through the vineyards and orchards in the country surrounding the resort, particularly in the spring when the red bud trees are in bloom.

Routes and Distances

Starting at the Golden Gate Bridge, the fastest route is to drive straight up U.S. 101 for 103 miles to the little town of Hopland. Pick up Route 175 and go east toward Clear Lake to the intersection with Highway 29. Turn right on 29 for three miles to Finley, where you take Soda Bay Road (also designated Route 281) to the left. Soda Bay Road makes a loop away from Highway 29 along the lake shore, past Konocti Harbor Inn,

Konocti Princess *cruises daily on Clear Lake*

and then back to rejoin 29.

The more scenic route, and also the best route from the East Bay cities, is to take U.S. 80 north to the intersection with Highway 29 at Vallejo. Follow it through Napa all the way to the lower junction with 281 on the west side of Clear Lake, seven miles past Lower Lake. Konocti is five miles past the junction. Between Calistoga and Middletown on this route is an eighteen-mile section of extremely steep, winding mountain driving. It is often slow, but the scenery is beautiful.

Accommodations

The Konocti complex includes 250 separate accommodations, and since many of these are large, family-oriented units, it is not unusual during the popular summer months for seven hundred to a thousand people to be at the resort. In the off-season it can handle conventions of up to six hundred.

Over half of the units are hotel rooms, each of which has two double beds, a dressing area with its own lavatory, and a bath with a stall shower. (There is no extra charge for children under twelve in these rooms.)

In addition to the regular rooms, there are a large number of very popular apartments. Each of these has a fully equipped kitchen, a large living room with either a queen-sized hide-a-bed or two single couches that make into beds, a bedroom with single beds (a few units have kings), and a full bath with a tub and shower. Each of the apartments also has a large, private, screened porch overlooking Clear Lake, while on the other side of the building are courtyards shaded by giant walnut trees and equipped with picnic tables and barbecues.

Konocti also has six beach cottages right on the lake. Even though these units, each of which will house four people, are rather rustic, they have their own lawn and picnic area and border on a beach, making them particularly suitable for families with children and correspondingly much in demand.

Activities

Since Clear Lake is the focus of much of the activity at Konocti, a large marina, adjacent to the lodge, is in full operation on a year-round basis. In addition to providing gas and ramps for launching boats, it also rents every type of boat as well as waterskiing and fishing gear. The *Konocti Princess,* an old-fashioned paddle wheel ferry, is another attraction at the marina. It takes guests on daily excursions around the lake, stopping at historical points of interest. During the summer season, it also goes on moonlight cruises on which cocktails and a light supper are served.

The smooth water of this twenty-five-mile lake makes it a favorite spot for water-skiers throughout the spring, summer, and early fall. Fishermen enjoy it, too, as it supports a wide variety of fish, including

One of Konocti's two large pools

largemouth bass, lake trout, crappie, bluegill, and catfish. For those who prefer swimming in the lake, the sandy beach below the cottages is a perfect place to go. Most of the resort's swimmers and sunbathers, however, prefer the two Olympic-sized pools located right at the water's edge. They are adjacent to each other and ringed with cabanas and large deck areas.

Looking toward Mount Konocti from the pool area, you can see the tennis courts. In a most unusual arrangement, the eight well-kept Laykold courts, no two of which are on the same level, are carved into the hillside amidst a profusion of plantings. These courts, each with a panoramic view of the lake, see a lot of action because tennis is popular at Konocti. Each one is lighted, too, and can be used well into the evening, which is an advantage in summer when it is sometimes too hot to play in the middle of the day. There is a small daily fee for using the courts.

Konocti is surrounded by golf courses—five in the vicinity and two excellent ones just minutes away. Buckingham Golf Club, one and a quarter miles to the north on Soda Bay Road, is a rather flat nine-hole course that completely circles a small lake. By contrast, the nine-hole course at the Riviera Golf and Yacht Club, a few miles to the south, is nicknamed "Cardiac Hill" because of the spectacular rise and fall of its terrain. It is worth noting that Konocti not only puts together attractively priced packages for golf and tennis, but also has special rates for fishing holidays.

The Pee Wee Golf Course on the hill just across from the lodge is one of Konocti's most amusing attractions, especially for kids. A sort of miniature Disneyland, it is filled with giant replicas of prehistoric beasts and fairy-tale characters. Some are there just for effect, while others, when properly hit, swallow the ball and propel it on to the next hole.

Bicycling is a favorite way of touring the quiet rural roads that lead through the extraordinarily scenic countryside. Hiking the trails around Mount Konocti is an equally popular endeavor. For rock hounds, the area is a paradise. Scattered through the valleys and creek beds of this lake country is an abundance of onyx, jasper, obsidian, and the famed "lake country diamonds," semiprecious gems formed long ago by volcanic activity. These stones have a seven to eight rating on the Mohs' scale of hardness, compared with a ten for real diamonds, but they are hard enough to be used for precision instruments and can be cut and faceted to make jewelry that has much of the fire and brilliance of real diamonds.

Dining

Like everything at Konocti, the dining room is huge. It has to be to take care of the summer crowds and the off-season convention trade. In the evening, however, when the overhead lights are dimmed and each table has a candle flickering in its center, a sense of intimacy is achieved in spite of the room's size. This feeling is enhanced by soft music performed throughout the dinner hour by an accomplished harpist.

Any of the entrées served at Konocti can be ordered a la carte, but the table d'hôte dinners are recommended. For a surprisingly reasonable price you will be served fine French onion soup, a dinner salad, an entrée (chosen from a wide selection), a beverage, and an excellent light dessert. As if this were not enough, you also will be treated to Souverain wine from the Sonoma Valley, compliments of the house.

The main lodge has a coffee shop, which is open all day and is perfect for breakfast or lunch. During the busy summer months, a snack bar by the pool serves the usual poolside fare such as hamburgers and hot dogs. On the other end of the pool, overlooking Clear Lake, is an attractive building known as the Oyster Bar. It, too, is designed to serve the sunbathers but with gourmet fare such as oysters on the half shell and exotic cocktails.

Several other viable dining alternatives are available in the area. The

Prehistoric monsters populate Konocti's miniature golf course

Riviera Golf and Yacht Club has one of the finest panoramic views of Clear Lake as well as an exciting menu. The small, intimate dining room is charming and during the cooler months has a fire glowing in the big fieldstone fireplace. It is open for lunch Wednesday through Saturday and for dinner nightly except Monday, with dinner dancing to live music on Friday and Saturday nights. On Sunday the feature is a lovely brunch.

In the other direction, just a mile or so from Konocti, lunch and dinner are served at the Buckingham Golf Club, although in winter, dinner service is restricted to Friday and Saturday nights.

A final suggestion for dinner is Robin Hill, which is about twenty minutes away in the direction of Lakeport and specializes in Italian food. The restaurant is housed in an old stone mansion with a great open staircase and stained-glass windows, and is filled with interesting art objects.

For explicit directions to any of these places inquire at the Konocti office.

Sea Ranch

Distances:
> From San Francisco—105 miles; allow 2½ hours
> From Eureka—206 miles; allow 5½ hours

Features:
> Actually a community of vacation homes; occupies a huge piece of seacoast property in a beautiful setting; offers a new concept in resort accommodations—visitors rent a full-sized house instead of a room or suite

Activities:
> Golf, tennis, swimming, strolling on ocean beaches, hiking, equestrian trails, scuba diving; abundant nature study and photography opportunities

Seasons:
> Year around

Rates:
> Houses—$42.50 to $100.00 per day with a two-day minimum stay; lodge rooms—$45 to $60 for two people

Address:
> Rams Head Rentals, P.O. Box 123, Sea Ranch, California 95497

Phone:
> (707) 785-2427 for house rentals; (707) 785-2371 for Sea Ranch Lodge

Houses dot rugged Sea Ranch landscape

Perhaps the most frequently asked question about Sea Ranch is "What exactly is it?" Well, it isn't a ranch. It is a town, incorporated by an association of homeowners, with its own post office, fire department, and administrative center. It all began as an ambitious development plan for ten miles of exquisite seacoast property in the northernmost part of Sonoma County. The idea was to build a community of privately owned homes that would guarantee tranquil and wholesome living conditions yet have the carefree flavor of a resort.

Today it is impossible not to be impressed with the quality of the development. At present there are 550 houses, but when driving through the area, visitors are aware of only a scattering of them. The extensive open spaces, many wooded preserves, controlled home designs, hidden auto parking, buried utilities, and protected beaches attest to the developers' respect for the environment.

Some of the houses are owned by full-time residents, but most are maintained as second homes and vacation cottages. To help mitigate the costs of ownership, about three-fifths of the houses are maintained in a rental pool, thus opening Sea Ranch to the general public like any other resort. The difference is that here you rent somebody else's fully furnished and decorated home. Each house is different, inside and out, and as with any home, each has a complete kitchen so that all meals can be prepared without going out (although there are restaurants in the area—see the "Dining" section).

When you come to Sea Ranch and settle into "your" house, you are granted all the regular owner's privileges for using the grounds and recreational facilities, and it takes but a short time to feel at home in the community. Under these conditions, those who like Sea Ranch often try a few houses first to find one they particularly like, then rent that one as much as a year ahead for future seasons. They also tend to stay longer, often renting by the week or month.

Nevertheless, there are almost always houses available on short notice for the weekend or in midweek, and since Sea Ranch is not too far from the major population centers, it can be a good spur-of-the-moment getaway.

Routes and Distances

Sea Ranch is located on famous coastal Highway 1, about a third of the way between San Francisco and Eureka. From San Francisco there are two ways to get there. The scenic route is to follow Highway 1 all the way—past Point Reyes, through Bodega Bay and Jenner, and along a final thirty miles of precipitous, narrow roadway. It is slightly faster to take U.S. 101 from San Francisco to Cotati, six miles south of Santa Rosa. At Cotati take Route 116 west to Jenner, then Highway 1 to Sea Ranch.

Sea Ranch is spread over ten miles and the house you have been assigned might be anywhere along its length. Stop first, therefore, to pick up your keys and instructions at the Rams Head Realty office. It is located midway through the area, near the fire station on Annapolis Road, which is well marked. Turn east when you come to the road and drive uphill about a half mile to the group of buildings containing the offices.

Accommodations

Having a complete house instead of just a room takes a little getting used to, but you quickly find it provides a degree of privacy and comfort that is difficult to match under usual circumstances.

The homes, the average age of which is five years, are scattered throughout this big property—some on the bluff and meadows above the ocean, and some back on the hillsides and in the forest. They invariably are modern and of every size and shape, ranging from cozy walk-in cabins to four-bedroom castles. All are completely furnished, and of course have kitchens fully equipped with dishwashers, all utensils, and dinnerware. Fireplaces and television are standard, and many houses have such special features as stereos, washers and dryers, and even hot tubs. All that guests must bring are towels and sheets. A few even allow pets.

People interested in one of these houses should contact the rental agency and explain the size, price range, and any special amenities they prefer. The agency will match their desires with the most suitable available house, then send them a packet of information about the house and the community, with a map showing the location of recreational facilities and the lodge. A fifty-dollar clean-up deposit, which will be returned if the house is left in the condition in which it was found, also will be requested. That, by the way, is what makes the system work: since each renter must clean up before departing, maid service (which would be difficult in such conditions) is unnecessary.

Not all the rental houses are in the Rams Head Realty pool, but if the agency should be sold out or have nothing suitable on its list, inquiries will be referred to another local agency. Also, for just a single night or two it might be preferable to stay at the lodge, which has twenty rooms, some of which have fireplaces, while most have lovely ocean views, and two even have their own private courtyards with hot tubs.

Activities

Sea Ranch's golf course is an exciting, relatively undiscovered course and reason enough for the committed golfer to come to Sea Ranch. It is rated number nine out of California's first forty courses, but could well be number one for both scenic beauty and difficulty. In its six-year existence, only six players have ever parred the course, and no one has broken par. One reason for the difficulty is that the links were designed in the Scotch manner, with roughs dividing the fairways.

Well-maintained trails lead everywhere about the property, making walking one of the best ways to see the area and enjoy the architecture and the magnificent terrain. One of the favorite trails closely follows the coastal bluff for about ten miles, affording many places to stop for a picnic and endless views of the ocean, seabirds, and sometimes seals and whales—all kinds of opportunities, in short, for nature study and photography. Occasional stairs or paths lead down to beaches. Other trails lead up and along the high ridge behind the property, passing through redwood groves and, at one point called "the hot spot," following a river-bank where there are fine places to swim when the water is high.

The Sea Ranch stables provide stall space and feeding twice a day for horses that people have trailered in. With many trails doubling as bridle paths and underbrush generally absent from the woods, riding is exceptionally good. (It is advisable to call the stable keeper ahead of time to reserve stall space.)

Tennis players can use three first-class hard-surfaced courts at the north recreation center, approximately midway on the property. A sign-up sheet is posted for making reservations for the next day's play. Adjoining the courts is a large swimming pool, a volleyball court, and a picnic area with barbecue pits.

It is probably obvious by this time that, because Sea Ranch is so spread out, an automobile is necessary to get from your house to the things

Hiking trail in redwoods behind Sea Ranch

you want to do. For this reason, private pilots should be warned that, even though air maps show an airstrip on the ranch, it is a bad idea to fly in because no transportation is available. (Some of the regular owners keep a "junker" car by the strip; otherwise, it gets only light use.)

Dining

The Sea Ranch Lodge, which includes a dining room and bar, is at the extreme south end of the property and is open daily for all three meals. The dining room affords good views and the menu has reasonable prices. Reservations are not accepted for small groups, however, which sometimes makes it necessary for guests to wait. If that happens, get your name on the list, then walk out to the bluff and look for sea lions or seals in the surf below until your turn comes up.

Ten miles in the other direction, across the Gualala River at the north end of Sea Ranch, is the town of Gualala, where there is a market, a deli, and three restaurants that serve dinner. Of the latter, St. Orres, located three miles north of the town proper, is the fanciest and most expensive. A Russian-style building topped with onion towers and decorated inside with extensive, intricate woodwork, it is worth visiting for the atmosphere alone, which is augmented by soft lighting, intimate seating, and fine French food. Reservations are necessary and are best made at least a day in advance.

Seals and sea lions often are seen in this cove below Sea Ranch

The next place to try is The Gualala Hotel, a yellow clapboard building occupying the prominent spot in the center of Gualala's one-block downtown. A good appetite is a necessity here. Quite the opposite from St. Orres, the hotel is not fancy, but the food is good and abundant. First, a big bowl of salad greens and a large platter of appetizers are plunked on the table. You could make a meal of these alone, but then comes a tureen of delicious soup from which you ladle your own portions. The entrée, which is the only thing you order, comes next, followed by coffee and a selection of desserts. The way the food keeps coming makes this an unusual dining experience, but the prices are reasonable. Reservations are not always necessary but are a good precaution.

The other place to eat is the Rusty Anchor, also in Gualala and also unpretentious. It offers an extensive menu of seafood and steaks for relatively modest prices.

Other than these there is always your own kitchen in your own house, possibly the best choice of all.

Northwood Lodge

Distances:
From San Francisco—70 miles; allow 1½ hours
From Santa Rosa—25 miles; allow ½ hour

Features:
The Russian River is a favorite vacationland relatively close to major population centers; Northwood Lodge, at midpoint on the river, is a good place to stay while exploring the area

Activities:
Golf, pool and river swimming, "hot tubbing," fishing, hiking, canoeing, picnicking; tennis nearby; touring Sonoma County

Seasons:
Year around; heavily booked May through October, plus all year-end holidays; more relaxed November through April; particularly beautiful in fall

Rates:
$37 to $82 for two people

Address:
P.O. Box 188, Monte Rio, California 95462

Phone:
(707) 865-2126

Northwood Lodge and pool

Sonoma County's lower Russian River terminates at the sea at Jenner after having followed a twisting course along banks thick with redwoods, cutting its way through the Mendocino highlands all the way from Healdsburg. Upriver from Healdsburg the character of the land changes, the valley opens out, becoming much wider, the redwoods occur only in occasional groves, and vineyards sprawl everywhere on the hillsides to supply the dozen wineries scattered along the upper valley's length.

The lower valley, where Northwood is located, is long on history and tradition. The frequent small towns along its crooked way bear witness—with such names as Duncan Mills, Mesa Grande, Monte Rio, Korbel, and Guerneville—to times past when the area was dominated in turn by Russian, English, Mexican, and finally, American influence.

The lower valley has been popular with San Franciscans as a vacation mecca since the turn of the century because its beautiful natural setting and the recreational opportunities offered by the clear, quiet river are so close to the city. Accordingly, the banks all along this part of the river are dotted with vacation homes, ranging from simple cottages to elaborate estates. In the middle of all this is Northwood, located halfway between Guerneville and Monte Rio. Its L-shaped main building, which surrounds a lovely swimming pool and lawn covered with planting boxes overflowing with color, is set in a clearing wide enough to have plenty of sunshine, though it is densely bordered by tall redwoods. Across the parking lot to the east is the Northwood Golf Course, which also is bordered by rows of giant trees.

In fact, anyone who is worried that the redwoods are dying out in northern California will be heartened by a visit to Northwood, where the grounds and much of the surrounding valley are thick with these rapidly growing second-growth trees, many already measuring three feet in diameter and a hundred fifty feet in height—solid evidence indeed of the regrowth potential of this hardy species.

Routes and Distances

From the Golden Gate Bridge, take U.S. 101 north to the junction with Route 116 at Cotati, or a little farther to the junction with Route 12 at Santa Rosa. Both 116 and 12 lead to Sebastopol. Go through Sebastopol to Guerneville, and beyond Guerneville for two miles. Then start looking for the Northwood Golf Course and Northwood Lodge signs on the left.

The more scenic way to get to Northwood is on Highway 1 through Bodega and Bodega Bay to Jenner. At Jenner, go east on Route 116 and find Northwood one mile past Monte Rio.

Accommodations

The lodge and the golf club at Northwood are actually separate entities, but they are so close together and complement each other so well—the lodge with the rooming accommodations and the club with a dining room and bar—that guests think of them as a unit.

Northwood cabins among redwoods

Northwood Lodge offers two kinds of accommodations: hotel rooms and cabins. Twenty hotel rooms are located in the lodge's main building, and all open to the pool and are clean and neat but not fancy. They vary considerably in size. The least expensive are small, with space for a queen-sized bed, a lounge chair, and a small writing desk. The bath has a shower but no tub. A variation of this room is called a housekeeping unit and includes a small kitchenette in an alcove. The next size is similar but has more room to accommodate two queen-sized beds. Some of these larger rooms also have kitchenettes. The largest hotel rooms are more amply furnished and have king-sized beds and full baths with tubs. All twenty units are equipped with color televisions hooked to a cable, which brings in excellent pictures. There are no telephones.

The cabins, which are set back among the redwoods, are considerably more spacious and comfortable. Each is really a complete little house, with a queen-sized bed in the bedroom, two bunks in an alcove, a bath with a tub, a living area with a fireplace, a kitchen, and a barbecue and picnic table outside. Two of the cabins are situated next to a second swimming pool, which they have practically to themselves. The other six have the advantage of being close to the hot tub deck, which is in an enclosure open to the towering redwoods and the sky. You must put a quarter in the slot to operate the hot tub's jets, but it is a small price for a very pleasant experience.

Activities

Sonoma County not only reeks of history, but also is naturally divided into several distinctive geographical areas, each of which is fun to explore. Northwood Lodge has the advantage of being centered among all of this and is not more than an hour's drive from any major point of interest.

The best way to enjoy Northwood is to divide your time between enjoying the resort itself and taking short trips into the surrounding countryside. Play a round of golf in the morning, for instance, then go out to Jenner for lunch and devote the afternoon to driving along the Sonoma coast.

The golf course is a neat nine holes, with 3,068 total yards, rated sixty-nine for men and seventy-one for women. It is a pretty course that occasionally produces disconcerting bounces when drives drift off the fairways and hit one of the big bordering trees. Usually not crowded, this course has some challenging holes and is acknowledged as fun to play.

The town of Jenner is less than a half hour from the lodge, on Route 116, which closely follows the Russian River until the river empties into the Pacific. Now a tiny fishing village, Jenner was once an important sawmill town and port for the exporting of redwood lumber. You can eat lunch at a restaurant called Jenner-by-the-Sea, then tour up or down the coast. To the north are the old Russian outpost of Fort Ross, now restored, and the

Foursome teeing off at Northwood golf course

Kruse Rhododendron Gardens. These serve as destinations, but the important thing to see is the indescribably rugged coast, which the narrow, twisting highway faithfully follows.

The road is even more precipitous to the south, passing through the long narrow strip forming Sonoma Coast Park before arriving at Bodega Bay. This quaint town fronts on the only safe harbor along the whole north coast and is the base for a sizable fishing fleet. The chapter on Bodega Bay Lodge explains in detail what you can do and see there.

Another day's diversion at Northwood might begin typically with a game of tennis at neighboring Monte Rio, a mile from the lodge. Two good hard-surfaced courts, maintained by the city parks department, can be found just behind the firehouse, to the left after crossing the bridge into town. The courts are free, and if they should be occupied when you arrive, you can warm up on two adjacent hitting alleys while waiting. After tennis, freshen up with a swim in one of the lodge's two pools, then set out on Route 116 in the other direction. Your destination this time is the town of Sonoma. Drive to Sebastapol and take Route 12 from there on a long, looping swing past Santa Rosa into the Valley of the Moon. At the end of the valley is Sonoma, where there is much to see and do, as well as nice places to eat, all around the picturesque town square. A monument marks the spot where the Bear Flag was first unfurled when the California Republic was declared. Since six other flags have flown over the region at

Swimming beach on Russian River

one time or another, there also are other historical monuments, as well as the restored homes of famous people, to visit. Return to the lodge via the same route, passing by an interesting string of "hot spring towns" and a number of nice parks and wineries.

A final exploratory trip is to go north along the upper Russian River valley through Healdsburg, Geyserville, and Cloverdale. This is wine and lumber country, with a dozen wineries, many redwood groves, and several sawmills to visit. From Guerneville take the West Side Road, which leads directly to Healdsburg. For a full day's outing, make a loop out of this same trip by heading west from Geyserville on the lovely Skaggs Springs Road, crossing the Mendocino highlands to the sea at Stewarts Point, then returning down the coast to Jenner. Geyserville, as the name implies, is the location of California's famous natural steam vents, and the site of much interesting experimentation in the development of geothermal power.

Driving trips are probably not for everyone and there is plenty to do right in the lower valley close to the lodge. The Russian River is broad and flat here. Steelhead come up in the winter, and in summer there is good swimming and picnicking at a beach under the Monte Rio bridge. Two agencies offer rental canoes, providing the opportunity to paddle upriver and then drift lazily back down while examining the vacation homes and estates along the way. A short distance north of Guerneville, on the Woods Road, are two parks full of giant old-growth redwoods and many hiking and picnicking opportunities. The Korbel winery, famous for its premium champagne, is two miles farther to the east on the West Side Road and welcomes visitors. Close to the winery is a hiking trail up to the Mount Jackson lookout, which affords nice overall views of the lower valley.

The problem at Northwood, in short, is not what to do but how to get in everything you want to do. It might take a return trip, or two, to do it all!

Dining

Food at the golf course clubhouse, which is across the parking lot from the lodge, is generally good and the premises pleasant, with a long bar along one side of the dining area and a view of the first tee of the golf course. During the summer season, dinner is served Tuesday through Sunday and luncheon Tuesday through Saturday. On Sunday, the clubhouse puts on a popular brunch that draws people from all around the neighborhood. In winter, the clubhouse sometimes is closed during the week and open only on weekends, but this schedule varies depending on the weather and amount of activity in the lower valley.

There are plenty of other places to eat in this area, some fairly close by. A favorite is Angelos, on the opposite side of the river about ten minutes from the lodge. To get there, go across the first bridge to Monte Rio, but before crossing the second bridge go left along the river road. Keep to the left, past the Village Inn and a dense stand of redwoods, until you come to the restaurant. Its atmosphere is informal and the cuisine Italian, with excellent specialties such as sautéed sweetbreads and chicken livers, all at reasonable prices. "Bar entertainment" is provided by a family of raccoons that eats spaghetti that the bartender puts out on a tree platform outside the window. It is a popular show that entices most of the restaurant patrons away from their tables while it goes on.

Burdon's, on the main street of Guerneville, is another well-liked restaurant, only a few minutes from the lodge. The River's End and Jenner-by-the-Sea are both located in Jenner and are considered to be good, with The River's End having the edge because of its view and atmosphere.

About two miles west of Monte Rio there is a right turn off Highway 116, which leads to the very small community of Cazadero. Small as it is, Cazadero's Cazanoma Lodge is generally acknowledged to provide the finest dining in the area. The atmosphere is that of a hunting lodge and the cuisine is old-country German. Be sure to call ahead for a reservation so you do not miss the experience of at least one dinner here.

Chanslor Ranch

Distances:

From San Francisco—67 miles; allow 1½ hours

From Eureka—250 miles; allow 5½ hours

Features:

A seven-hundred-acre working cattle and sheep ranch within easy riding distance of the sea; limited accommodations for not more than twenty guests, who enjoy close personal attention from the proprietors

Activities:

All equestrian activities; observing, and for those so inclined, participating in ranch operations; exploring the Bodega Bay, Russian River, and north coast areas

Seasons:

Year around, with limited dinner schedules in the winter season

Rates:

For two people in ranch house—$43 to $49, including breakfast; special $28 bed and breakfast rates available on weekdays during off-season. Bunkhouse, with accommodations for up to twelve —$41 to $65, depending on season and time of week (rendering cost per person low, depending on number). Riding and dinner charged extra; no lunch is served

Address:

P.O. Box 327, Bodega Bay, California 94923

Phone:

(707) 875-3386

Modest Chanslor Ranch bunkhouse

This is the smallest and most specialized of the resorts described in this book, but enough people enjoy horses and western life to justify its inclusion. If you are one of those who love horses and like to ride, Chanslor Ranch may be your kind of place.

This ranch is impossible to discuss without talking about its proprietors, Bonnie and Bob Hardenbrook, because they make it what it is. Bonnie oversees operations and Bob is the gourmet cook who runs the kitchen and prepares the dinners. In a way, what the Hardenbrooks do is a labor of love. Some time ago they abruptly changed their lives and got out of the city rat race, quitting good jobs, changing course 180 degrees, and taking the plunge into ranching. The ranch is a big working spread with lots of animals; the guest part of the operation seems to be almost a side-line, except that the Hardenbrooks take such care, and obviously enjoy, making visitors from all over the country feel like friends in their home.

Chanslor Ranch is the kind of place where everyone quickly gets to know everyone else. The custom is to gather in the living room of the ranch house before dinner and have a glass of wine, listen to music, and get acquainted with the other guests. Everyone eats dinner together, and the hosts are ready to talk at length about Morgans versus Appaloosas, bloodlines and breeding, training and shows, or the interesting people who have visited them over the years.

Animals, particularly horses, are what make a ranch of course. The

Hardenbrooks have a particular fondness for the noble-looking Morgan, although their stable also includes quarter horses and standard breeds. The ranch sits at the base of rolling, nearly treeless country that is well suited to sheep, so there are a lot of sheep around, as well as some cattle, milk cows, many cats, and a couple of black dogs. And as deer thrive under the same conditions as sheep, it is not unusual to look out the ranch house window at dark and see a dozen or more of these wild animals browsing just beyond the fence.

Chanslor Ranch, in short, is small, specifically oriented, and an unusually personal place. It either fills a person with delight or it misses entirely. You should be able to tell from this chapter if it is for you.

Routes and Distances

Chanslor Ranch is two miles north of Bodega Bay on the east side of Highway 1, with a large, easily seen sign marking the entrance. Coming from the Bay Area, follow the same directions as for Bodega Bay Lodge.

There will be some who find it convenient to approach from the north, however, and these will be rewarded with a spectacular sight-seeing experience along 150 miles of cliff-hanging seacoast highway. It is possible, of course, to take the inland route, U.S. 101, from Eureka through the redwoods to Santa Rosa, then head west twenty miles on Route 12 through Sebastopol to Bodega Bay. This is quicker, much of it on freeway, but by switching to Highway 1 at Leggett and allowing a few extra hours (and hoping for a day without fog), you will see an incomparable stretch of country that will demand later revisiting, which, in fact, is a major activity for guests staying at the ranch.

Accommodations

Visitors to Chanslor Ranch must be warned not to expect an imposing layout. Much the same as any moderate-sized farm, it has only three main buildings: a modern ranch house, a bunkhouse, and a big white barn, plus the usual scattering of small outbuildings, all surrounded by white board fencing typical of horse country. The ranch house itself contains only three guest rooms. They are bright, clean, and pleasantly furnished, each with its own large bath. These are the desirable accommodations, and are always filled first.

The bunkhouse is aptly named. A wood frame building, it has two big, plain bedrooms (each of which sleeps four), a simply furnished common living room, two utilitarian baths, a bunk room with four bunks, and a kitchen. The whole thing can accommodate twelve people. It usually is rented as a unit, and on a weekly basis during the summer, although the two bedrooms can be rented separately when they are available and the ranch house is full. The ranch house is most comfortable, however, so first ask for accommodations there.

Chanslor Ranch guests set out through dunes

Activities

A typical day at Chanslor Ranch goes like this: the guests arise in the morning and drift over to the ranch house, where they have a leisurely breakfast at the same big table where they had dinner the previous evening. Meanwhile, the wrangler can be seen through the window, currying and saddling horses in front of the bunkhouse. At 9:30 or 10:00, riders report to the line and have horses assigned according to each rider's ability. Then the wrangler, or sometimes Bonnie herself, leads the group either through the dunes to the ocean or up one of the brushy draws into the bare hills to the east. In either case, everyone has opportunities to practice horsemanship, and doing the kind of riding he or she or it likes best—long trots or canters, or just walking—and to observe the wildlife, which includes deer, rabbits, swans, ducks, and the many shorebirds that abound everywhere in the region. About two hours later the group returns and everyone scatters for lunch (see the "Dining" section), and the afternoon's diversions.

After lunch, some come back to the ranch. There are those who like to pitch in with the workaday chores. Others who want to do more riding take special rides that can be organized in the afternoon. Music lovers take delight in the Hardenbrooks' impressive collection of records and tapes, and others browse among the books, magazines, and scrapbooks in the ranch house library.

But most guests devote the time between lunch and dinner to exploration. Those who lunch at Bodega, for instance, go on to visit the art galleries (the restaurant itself at Bodega doubles as a gallery) and the craft shops for which the town is known.

Bodega Bay, on the other hand, is a fishing village where it is easy to spend hours watching the commercial activity along the waterfront. For a change of pace, people interested in contemporary residential architecture find that the whole south end of Bodega Bay is a world apart from the village and a fascinating showplace, full of outstanding examples of unusual designs.

To the south of the village is Doran State Park, with a fine long beach and a jetty from which to fish and look for sea lions, while to the west lies Bodega Head, a large bird-sanctuary and the site of the University of California's Marine Biological Laboratories (which conduct public tours on Fridays).

Those who go north to Jenner for lunch can continue on along the "abalone coast," a favorite area for scuba divers, whose vans often dot the roadside, or they can go east up the Russian River into an enchanted area of redwood forests and streams. Should you decide on the latter, first spend a few moments looking at the Hardenbrooks' scrapbook about the times when Russian settlers were vying with Mexicans and the British for control of this part of the coast. It is an absorbing but little-known story, and many artifacts from the period are still intact, including the old Russian outpost of Fort Ross, now completely restored and open for inspection.

Finally, many of Sonoma County's famous vineyards and wineries are but a short drive from the ranch. The Hardenbrooks know where the little operations are, tucked away in the hills, and are glad to prepare self-guided tour schedules for any guests who want to discover new vintages.

Dining

Although breakfast at the ranch is provided as part of the room prices, it is in no way an ordinary continental breakfast, but rather a real ranch meal, with homemade biscuits, marmalade and jam, fresh melon, bacon, eggs, and coffee. (Coffee also is kept on the buffet all day for anyone who wants it.)

Because people tend to scatter after the morning ride, luncheon is not provided at the ranch. The favorite places to go instead are Murphy's Jenner-by-the-Sea at Jenner, the Tides Restaurant in Bodega Bay, and The Gallery Restaurant, located in a nostalgic frame schoolhouse in Bodega.

Dinner is the highlight of the day at the ranch. Serving time is 7:30, with everyone turning up early for the social hour preceding the meal. The ranch provides a tiny bar equipped with ice and a selection of mixers, and guests fix what they like, providing their own liquor. Time passes quickly as guests tell of the day's activities and swap ideas about what to do the next day. Everyone feels well acquainted when it is time to move into the

Bodega Bay waterfront

dining room, where a big fire is blazing in the fireplace. One of the guests is asked to select the music for the evening.

A typical dinner starts with a basket of fresh sourdough bread followed by a gourmet salad, which is often something unusual. The main course may be tender roast beef, with homemade herbed pasta and baked acorn squash stuffed with tiny apple chunks. Carafes of red wine are kept full at each end of the table. After the entrée is served, the hosts sit down and join the "family." This is a good time to get more information about horses, the history of the area, or where to go and what to see. At the end, you can expect a rich dessert, possibly chocolate fudge pie topped with whipped cream, and coffee, after which everyone moves back to the living room to read, play games, or chat some more.

It should be noted that the dinner schedule sometimes varies. Dinners are served most nights in summer and on weekends, or whenever during the winter enough people will be present to make it worthwhile. If the patronage is too sparse, however, you will be advised to go out. In that case, all the places listed for lunch are good, plus another favorite, The Rivers End Restaurant in Jenner, which is open only for dinner and is just a short drive away.

Bodega Bay Lodge

Distances:

From San Francisco—65 miles; allow 1½ hours

From Sacramento—104 miles; allow 2¼ hours

Features:

A comfortable base from which to explore the north coast; all rooms have fine views of the bay and ocean

Activities:

Exploring the coast, golf, bicycling, walking the beaches, fishing, observing commercial fish boat activity in the village, photography

Seasons:

Year around

Rates:

$54 to $60 for two people

Address:

P.O. Box 357, Bodega Bay, California 94923

Phone:

(707) 875-3525

Bodega Bay Lodge is low lying, unobtrusive

Highway 1 from San Francisco going north first strikes the Pacific coast at the little fishing village of Bodega Bay. From there all the way to Westport it runs close to the ocean, narrow and twisting up to countless headlands and down into canyons between. Without question, this is one of the outstanding scenic drives in the United States, and is a particularly fine destination for those from the Bay Area or the inland valleys who find themselves with time for a short getaway.

Located at the portal of this unique stretch of California's north coast, Bodega Bay Lodge is a logical headquarters from which to explore the area. Unlike most of our getaway destinations, this lodge has no restaurant or sports facilities of its own, but it makes up for this lack by its scenic location and by the interesting activities and restaurants that are found nearby. Situated on a low hill between the village and the Bodega Harbour Country Club, it overlooks the harbor on one side and the ocean on the other, with the long finger of Dorian State Park stretching out directly in front. Always quiet, with cheerful and pleasant rooms, it is a lodge—and an area—for the most vigorous as well as the most laid-back of vacationers.

Routes and Distances

The scenic route, for those starting at San Francisco or the cities south of there, is Highway 1, which crosses to the coast immediately after passing Marin City. When the highway reaches the coast it proceeds through part of the Point Reyes National Seashore. Should time allow, take a side trip there, driving out to one of the points for a short walk and possibly a picnic lunch. This large coastal preserve is believed to be inhabited by more species of birds, some quite rare, than any other single area along the California coast.

Should time be important, however, the quick way to Bodega Bay is to take U.S. 101 north to Petaluma and the Valley Ford Road west from there to where it intersects Highway 1 at Valley Ford. Drive three miles up the coastal highway to Bodega, then drive five more miles to Bodega Bay. Shortly before entering the village, look for the Bodega Bay Lodge sign on the left.

Accommodations

A favorite nonactivity here is relaxing on your private deck and watching the activities in the Bodega Bay harbor. The lodge is strategically situated on the first rise of land behind the sandspit that forms the bay, affording a fine view for every room.

This is the largest hostelry in Bodega Bay, with a total of forty rooms, all with telephones and televisions. Each of the rooms is relatively large and has a two-part bath. Live plants in the room and on the deck are a nice touch, as are the chocolate mints waiting on the dresser when you arrive. An electric pot and instant coffee also are provided. A queen-sized bed is standard, and a few larger rooms even have two. Nine rooms also have fireplaces, which are nice on foggy winter days. The units that do not have

Fishing vessels at anchor on Bodega Bay

fireplaces have kitchenettes instead. (No utensils are provided unless you notify the front desk that you want to prepare meals.) The fireplaces and number of beds determine the small price variations among rooms.

Activities

Bodega Bay is the only good harbor for small boats on the long coast between San Francisco and Eureka. With rich fishing grounds lying offshore in both directions, it is a natural center for commercial fishing, the main industry of the area. The village of Bodega Bay surrounds the bay on three sides with support activities for the fishing fleet, including buying wharves, ship chandleries, repair yards, docks, and moorages.

All this activity renders Bodega Bay authentically picturesque, in contrast with so many tourist towns that have been artificially reconstructed. Visitors poking about the waterfront can see how fish are unloaded and bought and what the boats and their equipment look like, and they can talk to the fishermen themselves. For photographers there are opportunities everywhere to get shots of boats at anchor and to sneak character studies of weather-beaten faces, or similar treasures, for their portfolios.

Another good way to enjoy Bodega Bay is to rent one of the lodge

Bodega Bay tallyman weighing the catch

Unusual architecture distinguishes Bodega Bay

bicycles and pedal around the area. An easy starting ride is to go out the long flat spit that constitutes Doran State Park and separates the ocean from the bay. On one side, big waves break on the beach, while on the other fish boats ply the sheltered waters of the bay. At the end of the spit is a long rock jetty from which you can fish without a license because the jetty is federal property and not subject to state taxes. The spit also is a good vantage point for watching boats going out to sea and returning, and also, for those who know the ropes, can provide an abundance of clams and crabs, which can be prepared in the kitchenettes back at the lodge.

Another bike ride is to go up to the country club grounds to look at the unusual architecture. This is hilly travel, but the houses are worth the trip. Architecture buffs who have traveled the coast and enjoyed the New England–style nineteenth-century restorations in Mendocino will be struck by the contrast between those prim, white Victorian houses behind their picket fences and the severe modern forms that hug the bluffs overlooking Bodega Bay.

A new attraction in this area is the country club's championship golf course, now open for public play. Beautifully kept, it offers an ocean view from most of its nine holes and is ranked as one of the most formidable of courses in California. For the benefit of golfers, the lodge cooperates with the country club to arrange attractive golf-and-lodging package plans. These change from time to time, so golfers should inquire when making reservations to find out what is currently available.

With all of this, touring the area—especially the north coast, the Russian River, and Sonoma County's wineries—remains the most popular activity for visitors here. To get an overview of the area, drive north to Jenner, then take the River Road along the Russian River to Healdsburg, go from there up the highway along the valley to Cloverdale, then cross to Albion on the coast and come back down the coastal highway to the starting point, allowing at least five hours for the total trip.

Dining

No food service is available at the lodge, but the people at the desk will recommend places to go as well as make reservations for you. The closest place, and one of the best, is the Tides Restaurant in Bodega Bay. Located in the middle of town, just a few minutes from the lodge, it is built on a wharf that it shares with a fish market. The Tides has a lively long bar (much favored by local fishermen), which adjoins the big informal dining room where the window tables look directly out on fishing vessels tied up alongside. The menu offers every kind of seafood, from sand dabs to lobster. One particularly fine specialty is the whole cracked crab, served on a platter with a hearty green salad and warm French bread.

Another nearby restaurant is Russo's, on the highway at the far side of Bodega Bay. It is for those who like good Italian food, have big appetites, and like to eat early, because Russo's caters to the locals and closes at 7:30 P.M.

Neighboring towns also offer good places to eat. The Rivers End Restaurant and Murphy's Jenner-by-the-Sea are located ten miles north in Jenner at the mouth of the Russian River. The Bodega Gallery Restaurant, open for dinner on Thursday through Sunday in Bodega, is also worth a visit, as are two places in Occidental and one particularly good German restaurant in Cazadero. The lodge management will describe all of them to you in detail.

Hartsook Inn

Distances: 200 miles north of San Francisco, 81 miles south of Eureka, on U.S. 101 1 mile north of Piercy

Features: A complete inn with a restaurant; located on the Eel River in the heart of the redwoods

Rates: $25 to $34 for two people in cabins; $44 for housekeeping units, accommodating four people

Address: Piercy, California 95467

Phone: (707) 247-3305

The main inn building, which is just off the coastal highway, contains a large, inviting lobby-lounge and a big restaurant, which attracts many drop-in customers from the highway and is a meeting place for local people. The rooming accommodations are in cabins scattered among redwoods that rise high above them. Each cabin is different, has its own unique setting, and is modern and nicely kept up inside. Singles, doubles, and suites are available, all with full baths. Some also have kitchen facilities. Recreation in the area includes sunbathing along the Eel, swimming, fishing, and hiking on trails among the redwoods. The inn is open from 1 April through October.

Cobweb Palace

Distances: 175 miles north of San Francisco, 126 miles south of Eureka, on Highway 1 in Westport

Features: A vision out of the past in the middle of nowhere, for those who like unusual experiences

Rates: $29 to $45 for two people, including continental breakfast

Address: P.O. Box 132, Westport, California 95488

Phone: (707) 964-5588

Westport was a thriving seaport in the 1880s, with fourteen hotels and as many saloons. Today, less than a dozen buildings make up the whole town. The Cobweb Palace, the sole remaining hotel, has just six rooms. The two in front have their own baths and balconies overlooking the Pacific, two others have private baths, and the last two share an adjoining bath. Downstairs there is a quaint restaurant that serves full-course meals and a parlor bar decorated to resemble an old-time English inn. The ocean beach is across the street (Highway 1) and down a path. Beachcombing and walking the back roads are the two available activities here. The hotel and restaurant are open year around or when enough people have made reservations.

Mendocino Hotel

Distance: 148 miles north of San Francisco, in Mendocino
Features: A historical building and the central structure on Mendocino's main street; faces the bay
Seasons: Year around
Rates: $30 to $50 for two people (shared bath); $55 to $100 (private bath)
Address: P.O. Box 587, Mendocino, California 95460
Phone: (707) 937-0511

Like most everything in Mendocino, this hotel is a faithful renovation from the nineteenth century, when the gold, timber, and fishing industries were in their heyday and Mendocino was a rip-roaring boom town. According to the hotel's brochure, Mendocino boasted seventeen saloons and fifteen to twenty bordellos at that time. Today, all the booming business activities, and presumably the bordellos, are gone, but an insurge of artists, sculptors, craftsmen, and performing arts people has brought some business to replace them, helping to make this an unusually attractive place to visit.

The hotel is right in the middle of everything. It has twenty-six comfortable and attractive rooms, most of which share a bath "down the hall." Breakfast is included in the room rate. The hotel has an appealing dining room and bar, as well as the deservedly famous Garden Room Lounge.

Joshua Grindle Inn

Distance: 148 miles from San Francisco, in Mendocino
Features: Offers bed and breakfast in a well-kept, historic house; within easy walking distance of town
Rates: $45 to $53 for two people
Address: 44800 Little Lake, P.O. Box 647, Mendocino, California 95460
Phone: (707) 937-4143

Built in 1879 by its namesake, this New England-style house, so typical of many in the Mendocino area, has recently been renovated and converted into an inn. There are just five guest rooms—the Grindle, the Nautical, the Cypress, the Master, and the Library. The first two have views of Mendocino and the ocean, the last two are distinguished by individual fireplaces. All have private baths and are furnished with antiques collected by the owners.

It takes several days of strolling Mendocino and its beautiful beach to appreciate them fully, and the Joshua Grindle is a good headquarters from which to make the most of the area.

MacCallum House Inn

Distance: 148 miles north of San Francisco, in Mendocino
Features: A famous historic inn just one block off Main Street
Rates: $34.50 to $135, with special rates during the week in the off-season
Address: Albion Street, P.O. Box 206, Mendocino, California 95460
Phone: (707) 937-0289

MacCallum House is ornately adorned with gingerbread fretwork and wrought iron, as befits one of the landmark buildings of Mendocino's days of glory. This is a big establishment, as wayside inns go, with twenty-one rooms, some in the original house, some in outbuildings, and some in the old barn, which has been converted to apartments. Each room is unique—some have ocean views, some have Franklin stoves or fireplaces, some have their own little entrance to the garden. Most have a sink in the room but share a bath. Two have private baths and one has a kitchen. Take your pick. Continental breakfast comes with the room and is served in the library. At the management's whim, other meals are served occasionally.

Glendeven

Distance: 147 miles north of San Francisco, on the east side of Highway 1, between Mendocino and Little River
Features: A typical north-coast mansion that has been renovated and made into a bed and breakfast inn
Rates: $40 to $55 for two people
Address: 8221 North Highway One, Little River, California 95456
Phone: (707) 937-0083

Glendeven is beyond walking distance to Mendocino but ideally located for exploring all of the north coast by auto. It is a big, solidly constructed example of the architecture of the 1860s. By its appearance, it might have been imported directly from Gloucester, Massachusetts. It has six guest rooms on three floors. The upper Garret Room, because of its magnificent bay view, is the most expensive. Breakfast is delivered on a tray to guests staying there, and it has a private bath. Breakfast on a tray and a private bath also come with the Garden Room, which overlooks the garden. The other four rooms are paired to share baths and their occupants have breakfast in the sitting room, which opens onto the garden. In the evening, wine is served and a fire is lighted in the sitting room. Glendeven is closed for two weeks at Christmas.

Little River Inn

Distance: 146 miles north of San Francisco, on Highway 1, two miles south of
     Mendocino
Features: The largest of the wayside inns; actually a complete resort facility; long
     established and well known
Rates: $48 to $100 for two people in inn; $55 to $70 in cottages
Address: Little River, California 95456
Phone: (707) 937-5942

The original owner of this century-old coastal mansion had interests in lumber
and shipping, and built his dwelling on high ground from where he could watch his
ships. Today, the mansion houses the lobby, restaurant, and bar, and is surrounded
by an assortment of buildings that have been constructed over the years to provide
rooming accommodations. Individual rooms, suites, and cottages take up to 150
guests. The bar, as well as most of the rooms, has a nice view of the sea. The dining
room serves three meals a day and has a fine reputation.

The inn is on the opposite side of Highway 1 from the ocean, behind a
sheltering row of eucalyptus trees, with a path leading to the road, then on to the
beach. Just behind the main building is a nine-hole golf course. The resort is closed
for three weeks in January.

Victorian Farmhouse

Distance: 145 miles north of San Francisco, on the east side of Highway 1, just south of Little River
Features: A charming, small bed and breakfast house
Rates: $55 for two people
Address: P.O. Box 357, Little River, California 95456
Phone: (707) 937-0697

A favorite hideaway for honeymoons and wedding anniversaries, the Victorian Farmhouse is the smallest of our wayside inns. It has only four rooms, two to a floor, with each pair sharing a parlor with a fireplace as well as a nightly decanter of wine, courtesy of the management. Continental breakfasts are consumed at leisure in the parlors, although the honeymoon room has a blind hole-in-the-wall through which a tray can be passed if the occupants do not wish to come out. Furnished with antiques, the rooms are large and convey a feeling of bright, flowery cleanliness. Each has a private bath. This is one of a number of convenient places to stay while exploring the Mendocino coast.

Harbor House

Distances: 146 miles north of San Francisco, 161 miles south of Eureka, off Highway 1 in Elk
Features: A large, beautifully maintained old mansion on a high bluff; superb views
Rates: $80 to $110 for two people
Address: Elk, California 95432
Phone: (707) 877-3203

The tiny town of Elk (which has one store, one gas station, and a schoolhouse) was once a thriving port for lumber schooners plying the redwood coast. In those days, the local lumber company built this house as a residence and guest house for visiting executives. Appropriately it is constructed entirely of redwood. The exquisitely paneled lobby is a fine example of the craftsmanship of the day.

The inn has five rooms, equal in appointments and design with the lobby, and four cottages grouped close by. Each room has an individual bath and a fireplace. The inn is operated on the modified American plan, with rates including breakfast and dinner. The small dining room affords fine ocean views and good food. As it is a real hideaway on a remote section of the coast, it has no organized sports. It is closed between Thanksgiving and Christmas.

Timber Cove Inn

Distance: 90 miles north of San Francisco, on Highway 1, three miles north of Fort Ross

Features: An extravagant piece of architecture on a dramatic, isolated bluff overlooking the Pacific

Rates: $39 for smallest room, up to $100 for hot tub rooms

Address: North Coast Highway, Jenner, California 95450

Phone: (707) 847-3231

Timber Cove is the result of somebody's improbable dream. Its design and location, together, are a tour de force that new visitors will long remember. The massive building is modern and rustic all at the same time. Of its forty-seven redwood-planked rooms, most have fine ocean views, and many have fireplaces and sunken tile tubs that are part of the room itself, separated by only a draw curtain. Six rooms even have private hot tubs. There are no phones or televisions.

The lobby of this inn is a great cavern dominated by an indoor-outdoor Japanese pond passing under a window wall, with a walk-in fireplace at one end and a long bar at the other. Down a few steps from the lobby is a dining room (necessary here because there are no restaurants in the area), which also has a fine ocean view. No organized sports are available: walking the coast and canyons and contemplating the surf are the main activities and exercise.

Village Inn

Distance: 70 miles from San Francisco, ¼ mile east of Monte Rio
Features: A big, old, rambling building that is not ashamed of a few signs of
wear; a very laid-back operation on the south bank of the lovely Russian River
Rates: $18.50 to $40 (private bath) for two people; winter rates—three days for
price of two
Address: P.O. Box 1, Monte Rio, California 95462
Phone: (707) 865-2738

The downstairs lobby, the narrow stairway, and the upstairs lobby where you
sign the book (if you can find someone to check you in) make a strong impression
as you first enter this inn. All are cluttered with bric-a-brac and mementos from its
past, and if this should be late afternoon, you will hear music floating up from the
cocktail lounge downstairs, which is the favorite meeting place for local young
people. Of the fourteen rooms upstairs, thirteen share baths "down the hall" while
one elegantly possesses its own. The rooms either look out to the river or into thick
groves of redwoods. A narrow porch off the lower lobby on the river side is a
delightful place to sip a beer and read or doze in the sunshine. Breakfasts and
dinners are served daily in the small restaurant, which has a limited menu, but is fun
to experience.

The Wine Country

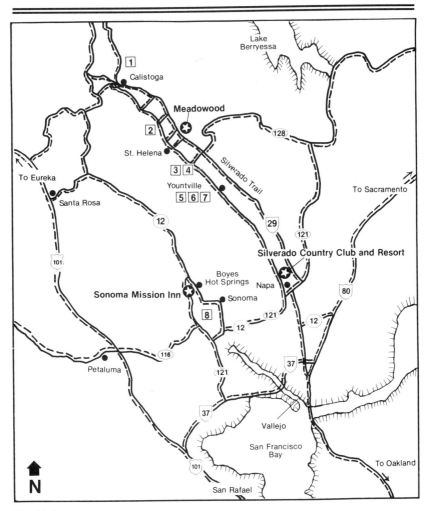

Wayside Inns

1. Calistoga Inn
2. Wine Country Inn
3. Harvest Inn
4. Chalet Bernensis
5. Webber Place
6. Magnolia Hotel
7. Burgundy House
8. Sonoma Hotel

Meadowood

Distances:

From San Francisco—70 miles; allow 2 hours

From Oakland—60 miles; allow 1½ hours

Features:

A small resort, hidden in the woods at the base of the Napa hills; seems remote, but is quite centrally located; comfortable and low-keyed, with friendly staff and complete resort facilities

Activities:

Golf, tennis, swimming, hiking, enjoying the Napa Valley's numerous activities—touring wineries, hot air ballooning, glider flying, mud baths

Seasons:

Year around except for 2½ weeks in January

Rates:

For two people, $90 to $110 midweek and $110 to $130 weekends; suites at the higher end of the price range can accommodate two couples, making cost per couple especially reasonable; no extra for tennis or swimming

Address:

900 Meadowood Lane, St. Helena, California 94574

Phone:

(707) 963-3646

Meadowood clubhouse overlooks golf course

Meadowood is one of the Napa Valley's best-kept secrets. Hidden among trees on a heavily wooded hillside just east of the lovely little town of St. Helena, it is in the heart of the wine country. The resort is small in terms of the number of accommodations, but it is large in terms of its facilities—a golf course, three tennis courts, and an Olympic-sized pool on over 250 acres of property.

The Meadowood property originally was developed some years ago as a private golf club, complete with a lovely clubhouse. Later on, tennis courts and a swimming pool were added as well as a limited number of guest accommodations for nonmembers—small chalets tucked into the hillside amidst the many evergreens and giant oak trees. Guests in these units, of course, were extended the privilege of using all the facilities during their stay at the resort.

In recent years, most of the vacationers flocking to the Napa Valley come to see the wine country, having been smitten by the romance and beauty of the industry. The imagination can be captivated by the wine making process—from the grapes growing in the vineyards through the intricate stages of making and aging the wine to the final product, the subtleties of which can be explored in the tasting rooms of the wineries.

Like any kind of sight-seeing, however, touring the wineries can get tiring and it is nice to have alternatives. Perhaps the nicest features of Meadowood are its location and the variety of activities it offers. For example, you can combine the pleasure of a round of golf or a tennis game with the wine tour activity. The quiet woodsy surroundings make pure pleasure out of a day of just lounging around the pool or relaxing in the sunshine on the deck of your little chalet. It is such a peaceful and beautiful spot that many guests find themselves coming back again and again, long after they have lost interest in how wine is made.

Routes and Distances

St. Helena is more or less midway up the Napa Valley, twenty miles north of Napa on Highway 29. From San Francisco, take U.S. 101 north to Highway 37, which skirts the north end of the bay and leads to Vallejo, where it intersects Highway 29 going north. Take 29 approximately thirty miles to St. Helena. From Oakland, go north on U.S. 80 to the intersection with Highway 29 and continue on 29 as directed above.

At the south end of St. Helena, look for Pope Street and go east on it about one mile, finally crossing a narrow stone bridge onto the Silverado Trail. Immediately jog left and then right to the Howell Mountain Road. Go about two hundred yards and look for the first paved street to the left off Howell Mountain Road. This is the Meadowood entry road, which takes you to the resort.

Accommodations

Early in 1980, shortly after being purchased by a new organization, Meadowood was extensively remodeled and refurbished, with utterly delightful results. Besides changes in the clubhouse at the golf course, each of the four chalets, which house the seven available guest units, was redone inside and out. When paint was sandblasted from the exteriors of the chalets, the rich native wood that was found underneath was treated with preservatives but was otherwise left in its natural state. Each chalet also has a spacious new deck across the front with a lattice roof overhang to provide partial shade in the sunny exposure.

There are basically two types of units. The larger ones consist of a living room confortably equipped with a large couch, a coffee table, a refectory table and chairs, and a wet bar, complete with a coffee maker, sink, and refrigerator. These units also have a large separate bedroom furnished with a queen-sized antique bed. If two couples wish to share the suite, the large couch in the living room makes into a comfortable queen-sized bed, and the bathroom is accessible from both the living room and bedroom. Two of the three units of this size have fireplaces in the living area.

The other Meadowood accommodations are studio units. Each one is a large room with antique furnishings, including a king-sized bed, overstuffed chairs, and a small dinette table and chairs. In addition, each has a dressing room, a bath, a wet bar, and a sun deck.

Two of the chalets consist of a single suite each, another larger chalet

Chalet perched on hillside at Meadowood

is a combination of a suite and an adjoining studio unit (this can be rented as a whole for six people or as two separate accommodations). The fourth chalet has three studio units, which open onto a common deck. Additional units are to be added gradually, but the quiet, low-keyed atmosphere that makes Meadowood such a pleasant retreat will be jealously guarded.

Because of fire codes, no cooking is allowed in the rooms, but when you open the refrigerator you will find a carafe of fresh orange juice for your breakfast, and at 8:30 A.M. a copy of the San Francisco *Chronicle* and a tray of hot croissants and sweet rolls will be delivered free to your door. How spoiled can you get?

Activities

Meadowood is one of those resorts where there are numerous things to do but no hassle or pressure about doing them. The three excellent tennis courts usually are available, but if they all are occupied, the wait normally is short and the time can be spent relaxing on the lawn around the swimming pool adjacent to the courts. There is no fee for using either the courts or the large pool as these are part of the privilege of being a guest at Meadowood.

Golfing on the resort's nine-hole links, on the other hand, does require a fee, but the course is seldom crowded, making it easy to arrange tee-off times to suit your convenience. This course is a great favorite in the

Meadowood pool in late afternoon

Napa Valley because it is so beautifully laid out, winding from the clubhouse through a series of forest-edged green valleys.

It is no problem to make a full day right on the Meadowood grounds. In summer a little snack bar beside the pool is open and in between swims people picnic on the grass beside the pool. Behind the club grounds hikers find pathways up to a ridge from which they can explore the backcountry of the Napa Valley. One short but invigorating hike is to take off cross country (there is no trail) straight up the steep hill behind the chalets. Keep on the high ground on the nose of the ridge all the way to the top. It is a hard twenty-minute walk, but you will be rewarded by the pretty groves of ancient oak and tremendous views of the valley in all directions. There also are many fine places for a picnic if you should happen to bring the makings along.

For further diversion, you can explore the wineries, restaurants, shops, and craft centers in the Napa Valley. Or you can go hot air ballooning, try soaring from Calistoga's airfield in a glider, or, if you are in the mood just to relax, go to one of Calistoga's several spas and treat yourself to a mud bath.

Dining

For guests in one of the chalets, dining at the resort involves strolling through the woods on a paved path to the clubhouse overlooking the golf course. In nice weather the tables are set outdoors on its wide veranda, shaded by big oaks. It is a pleasant place to eat, and it is a shame that presently the dining room is open only on weekends. The food is good, and although the menu is a la carte, it is reasonable in terms of total cost. It lists several unusual salads, with such entrées as a fresh fish of the day, shellfish selections, poultry, and a variety of meat dishes. The filet mignon with Madeira mushrooms is outstanding. So is the fascinating selection of wines—over 150 labels from sixty-one wineries—all from the Napa Valley.

Luncheon is served Wednesday through Sunday at the clubhouse for golfers and guests of the resort. During the summer months the poolside snack bar is open Tuesday through Friday.

Not far from Meadowood a variety of options for midweek dining are available. St. Georges, a new restaurant in St. Helena, is receiving very favorable comments. Located on the southern edge of town, it has a courtyard for private outdoor dining and serves fine continental cuisine. Those partial to French cooking will enjoy La Belle Helene in St. Helena, or can drive a few miles to Napa for a gourmet treat at La Baucane on Second Street. Mama Nina's in Yountville offers fine northern Italian cooking in an informal atmosphere. Also within easy range is the Silverado Country Club and Resort where a choice of excellent continental cuisine in the main dining room can be weighed against a fine dinner from the broiler in the new Royal Oak Restaurant. Perhaps one of the most romantic spots to dine is at one of the wineries. Domaine Chandon, on the west side of Yountville, is elegant, and the Souverain winery at Healdsburg is comparable. Both offer outdoor dining, weather permitting, and a lovely view.

Robert Mondavi winery

Silverado Country Club and Resort

Distances:

From San Francisco—50 miles; allow 1½ hours

From Oakland—40 miles; allow 1 hour

Features:

A large, beautifully maintained, premier resort; offers almost every conceivable service and amenity; located at the foot of the Napa Valley's famous wine country; includes two eighteen-hole golf courses, fourteen tennis courts, and eight swimming pools

Activities:

Golf, tennis, swimming, exploring the Napa Valley, bicycling; horseback riding, hot air ballooning, glider rides, waterskiing, antique shopping, gourmet dining all nearby

Seasons:

Year around; last half of November, December, January, and February are the "slow" months

Rates:

$89 for two people in spacious studio apartment with kitchenette; $125 in one bedroom suite with full kitchen; during winter season, these rates drop to $80 and $98 respectively

Address:

1600 Atlas Peak Road, Napa, California 94558

Phone:

(707) 255-2970

Silverado Country Club and Resort

For some reason, the very name Silverado stirs the imagination to romantic expectations, and if you are visiting there for the first time you need have no fear of disappointment. On entering its gates, you look down a long lane flanked with eucalyptus trees. In the distance is a beautiful old mansion, which was built shortly after the Civil War and is now the headquarters of the resort.

History tells us that General John F. Miller, a veteran of the war, and his wife bought the property and built this estate in the early 1870s. Having traveled extensively in Europe, they borrowed a little from the French and the Italians in designing their home and came up with a stunning result. Rolling lawn, studded here and there with date palms and colorful flowers, accentuates the beauty of the setting. Behind the mansion, along the terrace overlooking Millekin Creek, is a 250-foot-long stone wall built, over a period of many months, from the round polished stones of the creek. Over 100 years later it has nary a crack and is considered one of the finest examples of stone masonry in California.

After a colorful century in which four presidents, including Abraham Lincoln, and many famous Californians were involved in its history, this beautiful estate was sold in 1953 to developers, who began its transformation into an incomparable recreational area.

Today, Silverado is large, elegant, well established, and dear to the hearts of vacationers from all over the United States who love comfort, good service, and good food. Nothing anyone could desire seems left to chance—the management tries to ensure that each guest has a perfect time. If you need a reservation at a Napa restaurant or want to know where to shop for antiques, the resort's concierge will efficiently make all the arrangements and find answers to your questions. If you want to "do the wine country," a full-time expert, who is on the staff expressly to arrange tours and provide guidance, will help you make the most of the occasion. Tours also can be arranged of the best of the Victorian-era houses for which Napa is famous. Then there are golf and tennis professionals for those who want to brush up on their games and improve their techniques. These examples of the services available at Silverado—as well as the numerous acitivities—present but a few of the many reasons why the resort is ranked among the finest in the nation.

Routes and Distances

From the Golden Gate Bridge take U.S. 101 to eight miles north of San Rafael, where you leave 101 to skirt the north side of San Pablo Bay on Highway 37. Take 37 for seven miles to the junction with Route 121, which leads to Napa.

At Napa remain on Route 121 going toward Lake Berryessa, pass the town proper, and look for the Silverado sign on the left at the Atlas Peak Road. A short distance up Atlas Peak Road is the resort's entrance.

From the Oakland airport take Highway 17 north to where it merges with U.S. 80. Continue north on 80 over the bridge to Vallejo, then take Highway 29 to Napa. At Napa look for the Lake Berryessa signs and Route 121. Follow it to the country club as explained above.

Accommodations

The accommodations at Silverado are the quintessence of comfort and convenience. The many clusters of one- and two-story units each surround a common green and a swimming pool. Each of the individual units in turn opens onto the green, and many have private fenced-in patios on the other side of the building.

Although there are large accommodations, the ones suitable for a couple are the spacious studio units or the one-bedroom apartments. A studio is more than adequate, having a large room with a fireplace, table and chairs, and studio couches that the maid converts to twin beds in the evening. In addition, there is a kitchenette, a convenient dressing area, and a bath.

A one-bedroom unit is even more comfortable. A spacious living room, full-sized and completely equipped kitchen, large bedroom with a king- or queen-sized bed, dressing room, and bath comprise the floor plan of these units.

Whatever you choose, you will find every detail designed for your convenience. This includes the complimentary bottle of choice Napa wine you will find waiting for you when you arrive.

Activities

Silverado offers enough right on its own grounds to keep most people busy for a long time, but with the bonus of a concierge to arrange social activities and make reservations for you for some of the adventures available in the Napa Valley, you might find yourself doing everything from hot air ballooning to taking mud baths in Calistoga.

To begin with, Silverado is a golfer's paradise, with two beautiful courses making a thirty-six-hole championship layout on the hills of the thousand-acre resort. All action begins and ends at the clubhouse, which contains a complete pro shop and restaurant.

The tennis facility is one of the finest in northern California, making Silverado a popular spot for major tournaments. Fourteen courts recently have been constructed, fanning out from a modern new tennis center and pro shop. Lovely landscaping and umbrella tables and chairs make a pleasant spot for observers and players.

For those returning hot and weary from various athletic endeavors, six swimming pools are scattered throughout the condominium clusters. For other water sports, you can go to Lake Berryessa, which is just forty minutes away and is noted for its fine waterskiing.

Ten-speed bicycles, for rent by the main swimming pool at the resort, provide a marvelous way to see the surrounding countryside. Roads, which

Golf is paramount at Silverado

One of Silverado's six swimming pools

are specially marked and have a generous shoulder especially for bikers, go all the way to Yountville. Some guests enjoy exploring the wineries this way, as well as shopping in the quaint little villages and having lunch along the way.

When it comes to seeing the wineries, most guests take advantage of the outstanding wine tours arranged by tour director Joanne DePuy, a longtime resident of the Napa Valley who is extremely knowledgeable about its history and its primary industry. Half-day tours leave from Silverado every day in the morning and afternoon, with the individual groups choosing the type of wineries they prefer to visit. Some enjoy the large, well-known wineries where formal tours and tastings are conducted, while others have a penchant for the small wineries where they have a chance to meet the owners in a more intimate atmosphere.

Another adventure the Silverado staff is glad to set up is a horseback ride at the Wild Horse Valley Ranch, just a half hour away. This is a real working ranch from which the owners conduct rides into the distant Napa hills, where the terrain is reminiscent of Wyoming landscapes. A special event is the evening ride, featuring a steak barbecue dinner accompanied by red wine served around the campfire. Equally popular are the breakfast rides, which can be arranged for weekends.

These days the ultimate adventures in the Napa Valley are in the air: taking a glider ride from the Calistoga airport where a fleet of two-place gliders and tow planes await the visitor's pleasure, or a hot air balloon ride, courtesy of Adventures Aloft, which operates from mid-valley, close to Silverado. The concierge at the resort will arrange any of these trips.

The balloon ride is especially exciting, providing a bird's-eye view of the whole valley to passengers riding in a tiny wicker basket slung beneath

Silverado guests ready for takeoff in hot air balloon

a gaily colored, seven-story silken bag. Takeoff usually takes place in Yountville early in the morning, when the air is still cool. Passengers arrive in time to watch the inflation procedure, then thrill to the strange sensation of takeoff as the balloons gently rise to drift down-valley with the breeze. Each trip lasts about an hour and is celebrated with champagne at the end. Don't miss giving this sport a try!

Dining

The quality of dining at Silverado, whether it is in the main dining room, the Royal Oak Restaurant, or the golf club grill, is commensurate with the excellence of all the other features of the resort.

The main dining room is large and somewhat formal. Men are expected to wear jackets for dinner, although ties are not required. Its cuisine is continental, always with a fine variety of entrées. Sumptuous breakfasts and lunches are served here daily, except on Sunday, when the most popular meal of the week, an elaborate champagne brunch, is offered.

The Royal Oak is a new restaurant in a remodeled part of the building that features a limited menu of items from the broiler—steaks, lamb chops, prawns, and lobster—served elegantly along with a la carte salads and gourmet desserts. It has become a favorite spot, so make reservations early.

The golf club grill is favored by golfers and tennis players who appreciate a cold drink, a sandwich or salad, and an atmosphere in which they can relax in informal attire after a hard game.

The small towns along the valley abound with other interesting restaurants. One of the best, in Napa, is La Baucane, a little French restaurant in a tall, skinny house on Second Street. Soup, salad, and dessert are included with all its dinners. Try not to miss the turnip soup, the La Baucane salad, the Coquilles Saint-Jacques, and the strawberries in red wine—just a few special favorites. For a change of pace, try Mama Nina's in Yountville for good Italian food, or go to the Domaine Chandon, a winery famous for its fine champagnes, and also for its elegant luncheons and elaborate continental dinners. These are a few possibilities. The concierge at Silverado will be glad to help with other suggestions, and to make reservations.

Sonoma Mission Inn

Distances:
From San Francisco—40 miles; allow 1 hour
From Sacramento—82 miles; allow 1¾ hours

Features:
A large, elegant resort hotel set on lush grounds; boasts a European-style spa complex and an excellent French restaurant

Activities:
Health spa, swimming, tennis; exploring the historic town of Sonoma, touring wineries, golf, horseback riding, bicycling, hot air ballooning nearby

Seasons:
Year around

Rates:
$85 to $110 for two people in regular room; $130 in small suite

Address:
Boyes Hot Springs, California 95416

Phone:
(707) 996-1041; toll free in California (800) 862-4945

Sonoma Mission Inn

For a good many years the old Sonoma Mission Inn was a run-down building in a run-down neighborhood and seemed imminently doomed to the wrecker's ball. But because of one man's vision, it instead was opened in June 1980 as a grand hotel of which the Sonoma Valley can be proud. This transformation took place, however, only after the old relic, which was purchased for a mere $200,000, was given a face-lift costing about $7 million by an enormous crew that worked steadily for six months.

Today the inn, with its stucco facade painted an earthy pink and its steep roof made of red clay tiles, is reminiscent of a hostelry you might see in Spain or the wine country of southern France. Grape arbors, beautifully manicured flower beds, and a wide expanse of lawn embellish a portion of the seven acres of grounds around the inn. So does the unusual poolside area, with Arabian-style cabanas flanking one edge of the pool and large canvas umbrellas and fine lounge furniture grouped around the other end.

On entering the hotel, you can immediately see that the restoration is a classic. The floor of the immense lobby is paved with glistening tiles on which sparse furniture groupings, all done in muted tones, convey a feeling of austere elegance. At either end of the foyer, a wide, gracefully curving stairway covered with plush carpeting leads to two levels of guest accommodations, the decor of which, like the restaurants and other common rooms of the hotel, reflect the same fastidious taste.

The ultimate feature of the resort is the recently completed multimillion-dollar European-style spa, which has every conceivable facility for recreation and therapy. It is interesting that the original resort also featured spa activities. The area's hot springs and artesian waters were the reason the inn was built in 1922 (and again in 1929 after the first building burned down). During those early years, fashionable guests came by boat and stagecoach to Boyes Hot Springs to enjoy the waters. Later, when the railroad came in, the appeal was broadened and people of ordinary means started to come. Little shacks and houses sprang up on small lots and the area became rather seedy. As the Sonoma area fell out of favor as a prestigious place to spend a weekend, the hotel began to decline. This set the stage for a wealthy New Yorker, who had spent many of his boyhood summers in Boyes Hot Springs, to realize a dream—to buy the old inn and restore it. In doing so, he has helped the lovely Sonoma Valley, with its mild weather and booming wine industry, again become a prime competitor for the tourist trade that the Napa Valley, its neighbor to the east, has enjoyed for so long.

Routes and Distances

From San Francisco, take U.S. 101 north to Highway 37. Turn east on 37, go approximately eight miles, then turn left on Route 121. At the town of Sonoma, pick up Route 12 at the town square. Two and a half miles north, on Route 12, is the Sonoma Mission Inn on the left, just past the California National Bank Building. Look for the distinctive pink portals at the inn entrance.

From the East Bay cities, take U.S. 80 north to the intersection with Highway 29 at Vallejo. Highway 29 joins with Route 12 a short distance north of Vallejo. Stay on 12 from there on, through Napa and Sonoma to Boyes Hot Springs.

Accommodations

There are no elevators in the hotel, but baggage is not a worry because an alert young attendant will greet you at the entrance of the inn, direct your parking, and see you to your quarters, all with a helpful spiel about what is going on and where.

Even the uniforms of these attendants carry out a color scheme of basic earthy tones—tan, taupe, and a reddish clay—that is used throughout the hotel and is skillfully combined to create an unusual, sophisticated atmosphere. In all of the hotel's 105 rooms, variations of these tones are used either as the dominant or accenting colors, with pleasant visual results.

Each room has its own individual charm according to its outlook and furnishings. Some rooms overlook a wide sweep of sunny lawn with occasional pockets of shade from giant sycamore trees; others overlook the manicured gardens surrounding the pool and terrace.

All the rooms have beds with canopies made of heavy canvas and spreads to match, old-fashioned ceiling fans, and white plantation shutters on the windows. The baths are carpeted and modernized with new cabinets and counters, although many of the interesting old fixtures have been retained.

Guests have a choice of rooms furnished with twin beds, or queen- or king-sized beds, with a slightly higher rate levied on rooms with a king. A few small suites, known as country rooms, also are available for a higher fee. In the tradition of European hostelries, a continental breakfast served in the Grill Room or on the terrace is included in the room rate.

Activities

Winter in the Sonoma area is short and mild and many outdoor interests can be pursued pretty much on a year-round basis, but the spa complex is good insurance against any off-season malaise. The complex includes an indoor swimming pool, Jacuzzi, sauna, steam room, exercise room, and massage room, as well as a diet kitchen to serve those interested in keeping trim and fit. Weekly fitness programs, developed in the style of European spas, also are available.

The main outdoor attraction at the inn proper is the lovely Olympic-sized pool and the three Laykold tennis courts, which are lighted for night play and are kept in impeccable condition. The comfortable cabanas and furniture around the pool, as well as beverage service, make lounging and leisurely card games especially pleasant.

Pool and sun deck behind Sonoma Mission Inn

General Vallejo's Mexican barracks in Sonoma town square

Two excellent golf courses are within a short distance of the inn. The closer one is the Sonoma National Golf Course, less than five minutes away, while a fifteen-minute drive takes you to the Oakmont Inn links. Both courses are eighteen holes and require reservations, which the concierge at the inn can make for you on request.

The concierge also can arrange horseback rides at a nearby stable and order bicycles for those interested in touring the quiet rolling valley. The bikes will be delivered and picked up at the hotel on request. With a little advanced notice, the concierge also can arrange hot air balloon trips over the beautiful vineyards and farmlands of Sonoma Valley. (These trips require a minimum of four people.)

Probably the most popular activity of guests staying at the inn is touring the Sonoma Valley wine country, home of some of California's most famous wineries such as Chateau Jean, Sebastiani, Kenwood, and Souverain.

Guests who enjoy seeing local historical sights should make a trip to Sonoma and visit the town square. It is fascinating to stroll around the block and see the troop barracks where General Vallejo billeted his Spanish and Mexican troops so long ago, and the nearby Swiss Hotel (now a restaurant) that was the adobe of the general's brother, Mariano Vallejo. There are many other landmarks as well as little shops, boutiques, and restaurants. One of the shops, The Cheese Factory, is a pleasant place to pick up some cheese and bread for a picnic at one of the wineries.

Dining

The Provençal is the inn's elegant French restaurant, already notorious and boasting a four-star rating for its country French and northern Italian cuisine. Much of its quick success is attributable to the chef, who came to the inn from Paris after a stopover at one of New York's finer restaurants.

The atmosphere in the Provençal is rather formal and requires proper attire: jackets and ties for gentlemen and dresses or evening pantsuits for ladies. The dinners, served every evening from six to ten, are always a la carte, although there is a complimentary soup with each entrée. A good range of excellently prepared meat, fish, and salad selections is available. All the breads and pastries are made in the inn's own kitchen. The dining room also serves a very popular brunch on Sundays.

On the main level of the inn next to the pool is an informal grill where light, very pleasant complimentary breakfasts are available for guests anytime in the morning. Luncheons also are served in the grill, although on sunny days—and there are many of them—guests generally will be found eating alfresco under giant umbrellas on the poolside terrace. In the evening, when a bright fire is burning in the terrace fire pit, it is pleasant to sit under the stars on the terrace and listen to music while enjoying a cocktail or after-dinner espresso or cappuccino.

Just a short distance away in Sonoma are many other good places to eat. Right on the square, you will find Au Relais, which is a French restaurant; The Capri, which specializes in Spanish food; and The Depot, which features continental cuisine. And The Big Three Fountain Restaurant, just across the street from the hotel, is handy for anyone interested in something more substantial than continental breakfasts and light luncheons.

Calistoga Inn

Distance: 77 miles north of San Francisco, on the main street of Calistoga
Features: A bed and breakfast inn that offers the additional convenience of a restaurant and bar
Rates: $25 for two people
Address: 1250 Lincoln Avenue, Calistoga, California 94515
Phone: (707) 942-4101

The town of Calistoga is famous for the nearby wineries and vineyards, for its mineral hot springs and mud baths, and for the sport of soaring, all of which are easily accessible to guests of the Calistoga Inn. All its rooms share community baths, attesting to the age of this gracious facility. Continental breakfasts, included in the room rate, are served daily in the sitting room. Reservations usually are a necessity for dinner in the dining room because of its good reputation and popularity. A stroll to the other end of town will bring you to the airfield where you can watch tow planes take gliders aloft, or even hire a ride in a two-seater. And don't miss the mud baths across the street.

Wine Country Inn

Distance: 70 miles north of San Francisco, in St. Helena, two miles north of the town center
Features: An inn in a quiet location with a high reputation for hospitality, charm, and comfort
Rates: $60 to $88 for two people
Address: 1152 Lodi Lane, St. Helena, California 94574
Phone: (707) 963-7077

Unlike so many of the wayside inns in this guide, the Wine Country Inn is new and, accordingly, offers up-to-date comforts and conveniences. The owners spent much time, and still do, traveling in New England studying traditional inns and applying the best of what they learn to their own inn. There are twenty-five large rooms, each one unique, and though the buildings are new, the furnishings are beautiful antiques. All the rooms have private baths, half of them have fireplaces, and some have little private balconies or patios opening to the lawn. Continental breakfast is included in the room rate and is served in the common room, buffet style, or outside on a deck in fine weather. The inn is surrounded by vineyards, and neighboring country roads offer opportunities for many nice walks.

Harvest Inn

Distance: 68 miles north of San Francisco, on the south side of St. Helena
Features: A brand new project built on the edge of a working vineyard; offers sumptuous accommodations
Rates: $65 to $110 for two people
Address: One Main Street, St. Helena, California 94574
Phone: (707) 963-WINE

The Harvest Inn is a mixture of old and new features. It is a collection of Tudor cottages randomly arranged to simulate an old English village. Each of the twenty-four cottages has several rooms and suites, all of which are furnished with antiques or antique reproductions, such as pull-chain toilets. Many also have fireplaces, with wood supplied. At the same time, these quarters are modern, with wet bars, refrigerators, color televisions, and even telephones in the baths. The inn also features an outdoor heated pool and a separate Jacuzzi, as well as a big separate combination lobby and wine-tasting room in which a complimentary continental breakfast is served.

Chalet Bernensis

Distance: 68 miles north of San Francisco, on the southern edge of St. Helena
Features: Victorian-style bed and breakfast inn in the midst of the wineries
Rates: $44 or $48 (with shared bath) to $57 for two people
Address: 225 St. Helena Highway, St. Helena, California 94574
Phone: (707) 963-4423

Surrounded by porches and adorned with "gingerbread," this house was built in 1884 by a prominent valley winemaker and is typical of the way mansions for the well-to-do were built in those days. Rooms are upstairs in the old home, and next door, the former water tower building has been restored and remodeled to include four modern guest rooms, each with a private bath, fireplace, and air conditioning. Furnishings of all rooms are Early American, with lace curtains, doilies, and iron or brass bedsteads. The chalet even has its own antique shop. The Sutter Home Winery is just next door, vineyards lie behind the chalet, and the Louis Martini and two lesser-known wineries are not far away.

Breakfast is included in the tariff and guests are invited to "sip sherry in the sitting room, relax on the wide porch, and picnic on the lovely grounds." No pets or children are allowed and smoking is discouraged.

Webber Place

Distance: 60 miles north of San Francisco, in Yountville
Features: A very small bed and breakfast inn on a quiet, shady side street
Rates: $50 to $80 for two people
Address: 6610 Webber Street, Yountville, California 94599
Phone: (707) 944-8384

This inn currently has only four rooms, but the proprietor plans to add more. The Veranda Suite, on the first floor, is an absolute delight. It not only has its own little shaded garden patio, but also has a magnificent old-fashioned, oversized bathtub on a tile platform right in the middle of the bedroom. All of its exposed plumbing is polished brass, which matches the antique bedstead. Another of the rooms upstairs also has a tub, almost like a throne, mounted in the bedroom. (The proprietor collects antique bathtubs and the new rooms will have similar tubs.) Room rates include breakfast, and wine in the evening. Webber Place is open year around, but make reservations to ensure having a room on arrival.

Magnolia Hotel

Distance: 60 miles north of San Francisco, in Yountville
Features: Well-known, long-established inn; features a small, exclusive restaurant
on Friday and Saturday evenings
Rates: $60 to $95 for two people in main building; $105 to $115 in newer Garden
Court
Address: 6529 Yount Street, Yountville, California 94599
Phone: (707) 944-2056

Located in the middle of Yountville, the Magnolia Hotel is a fine headquarters
for leisurely making the most of all the attractions of the village and the
surrounding area. The hotel is bigger than it appears from the street due to its depth
and adjoining annex, called the Garden Court. Between the main building and the
annex, well screened from public view, are a private swimming pool and a hot spa
for the use of guests. All the rooms have private baths and are furnished with
antiques.

Over the years, the Magnolia Hotel has received much well-justified publicity,
but as a result it is usually full and often has to turn people away. Reservations well
in advance for both the inn and the restaurant are therefore always advisable.

Burgundy House

Distance: 60 miles north of San Francisco, in Yountville
Features: One of the Napa Valley's most famous bed and breakfast inns
Rates: Low season and high season rates vary widely from $40 to $90 for two
  people
Address: 6711 Washington Street, Yountville, California 94599
Phone: (707) 944-2855

Unlike the many wayside inns that have a Victorian aura, Burgundy House reflects French influence throughout. It was built in the 1870s by a wine maker who used fieldstones to construct its very thick walls. A huge stone fireplace in the Hearthroom, which is full of antiques and interesting memorabilia, is typical of the French style. Here, breakfast is served in the morning, and wine is savored before a fire on crisp evenings. (Both breakfast and the wine are included in the rates.)

This is an intimate place to sojourn, with just six rooms, each delightfully and uniquely furnished with antiques. The inn is centrally located in Yountville, but is off the main road on a quiet side street. The rooms, which look out over neighboring vineyards, tend to be cool in the summertime because of the twenty-two-inch-thick stone walls. A shady patio in the back, surrounded by pretty plantings, invites guests to relax.

Sonoma Hotel

Distance: 38 miles north of San Francisco, in Sonoma
Features: Historic small hotel in a historic location; recently restored and renovated
Rates: $35 to $55 for two people
Address: 110 West Spain Street, Sonoma, California 95476
Phone: (707) 996-2996

Spend a few days in the Sonoma Hotel, devoting your time to exploring the town and its vicinity, and you will come away an expert on California's early history, for Sonoma was the cradle of the original California Republic. The early Mission San Francisco de Solano, the old Mexican barracks (now a museum), the adobe home of General Vallejo, the Bear Flag monument, and the Blue Wing Inn are all within easy walking distance, as is the Sebastiani winery. Only slightly farther away are dozens of other worthwhile points of interest.

The hotel itself was built in 1872 and has seventeen rooms, four with private baths and the rest in the old style with the bath and showers at the end of the hall. Every room is unique and has nineteenth-century decor and furnishings, mostly antiques collected in the area. No food is served, but there are ample restaurant facilities on the square, where the inn is located.

The Houseboats

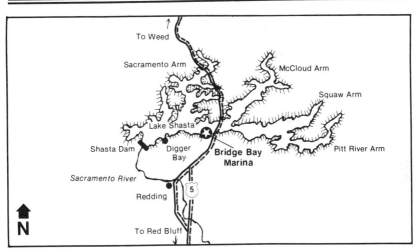

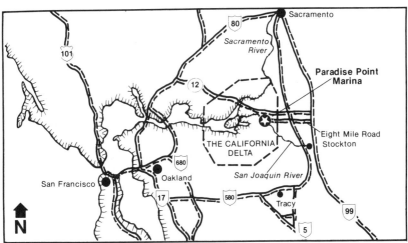

The Houseboats

Distances:

Paradise Point Marina (California Delta)—85 miles from San Francisco; allow 1¾ hours

Bridge Bay Marina (Lake Shasta)—230 miles from San Francisco; allow 5 hours

Features:

Fully equipped, spacious houseboats that actually are "floating resorts"; available for rent at two California locations; comfortable adventuring in a new type of vacation environment; suitable for both inexperienced and seasoned boaters

Activities:

Operating houseboat, exploring inland waterways, fishing, sunbathing, swimming, wildlife photography

Seasons:

Year around; 19 September to 14 May is off-season

Rates:

A number of rate schedules prevail depending on type of boat, time of week, and time of year. Following are sample rates. Smaller boats, three days—$310 to $335 off-season, plus gas; $450 to $475, in-season, plus gas. Larger boats, three days—$335 to $495, off-season, plus gas; $475 to $695, in-season, plus gas. Other lengths of time at proportionate costs. Note in figuring cost per person that boats sleep up to ten people.

Addresses and Phones:

Central Reservation Office, PlayMate Resort Marinas,
730 South Cypress, La Habra, California 90631
(213) 691-2235

Paradise Point Marina, 8095 Rio Blanco Road,
Stockton, California 95209
(209) 952-1000

Bridge Bay Marina, 10300 Bridge Bay Road, Redding,
California 96001
(916) 275-3021

Bridge Bay Marina on Lake Shasta

Sometimes a getaway is taken to have some well-earned fun and sometimes to relieve the mind of stifling routine. In either case, no change of pace is more abrupt and offers more unusual ways to have fun than taking off on a houseboat into unknown territory—on your own, with nothing but your whims for a guide.

Now it so happens that where the Sacramento and San Joaquin rivers come together, less than two hours from San Francisco, is a little-known area simply referred to as "the Delta." This vast piece of land is laced with a thousand miles of navigable waterways that are close enough to the Pacific to be influenced by tidal movements.

Farther north, at the other end of the Sacramento River (a few minutes north of Redding), Shasta Dam backs up the river's headwaters to form California's largest man-made lake, Lake Shasta. Located in pristine forest country, much of it inaccessible by road, the lake's waters reach far into the hills in a complex pattern of long, narrow arms. They form nearly four hundred miles of shoreline, full of coves, beaches, and private places where a boat can tie up overnight.

To explore these waterways, it is not necessary to own a yacht or trailer. On both the Delta and Lake Shasta you will find marinas with houseboats for rent—ready to go and provisioned with everything needed for cruising. The marina staffs can teach near novices enough within a half hour that they can step aboard and confidently put out to sea, captains of their own rig. Bedding and linen will be found aboard, so all the renters need to bring is food, clothing, and personal gear.

Arranging a houseboat getaway starts with a call to the rental agent, who will send a packet of literature describing floor plans of the various boats, with rate sheets, seasonal specials, and information about the area.

The rental price of houseboats is the same whether the rental party has two people or the maximum number the boat can hold. Therefore, the price per person is considerably reduced if the boat is full. The first consideration then, depending on the number of people that will be on the trip, is the choice of a boat. There are a number of sizes available. The smallest and least expensive are twelve feet wide by thirty-six feet long. There are several different models in this size, but basically they can sleep six aboard, maximum, and are thus called "six sleepers." The larger boats, also with a number of varying floor plans, are "ten sleepers," twelve to fifteen feet wide and forty-two to forty-seven feet long. The smallest boat, the "Fun Ship 6," has a compact "head" with a shower, an efficiency kitchenette, and daytime seating arrangements that make into beds at night. The ten sleepers are more commodious; some even have a bathtub, a wet bar, and a full-sized, U-shaped kitchen. In effect, the bigger the boat the more amenities are available, but all have plenty of storage space and room to move about.

The big decision is where to cruise—on the Delta or on Lake Shasta—and it is not an easy choice to make. The Delta offers more miles of waterways and more challenging navigation. Its myriad channels are confusing as they often are full of islands and have occasional false entrances that look very much like the right way to go, but are not. The Delta also has beautiful scenery, but much of the cruising is between high levees that permit little viewing of the countryside. The area is full of water life and there are many abandoned docks and floats where boats can tie up for swimming and fishing. And everywhere around the Delta there are little marinas that welcome visitors and provide such necessities as bait, fuel, and groceries. Many of them even have dockside restaurants.

Lake Shasta, on the other hand, has only a few marinas, although the Bridge Bay Marina, where you start, is centrally located and has a complete supply center with a general store, a snack bar, and a good dinner restaurant. It also has a motel, which is convenient for people who want to drive up in the evening, spend the night, then get an early start in the morning. Ringed with forests and mighty peaks, Lake Shasta offers a lot of beautiful territory for the houseboater to explore. Unlike the Delta, however, it does not have a confusion of islands and false waterways and so is easier to navigate. It also is well stocked with a variety of fish.

After studying the literature and making the necessary choices, you mail in the reservation form with a deposit to ensure that your boat will be ready. The marina sends back a confirmation, along with a booklet to inform first-timers about the essentials of boat handling, safety rules, and personal items to bring. From there, the adventure begins. Who knows where it will take you?

Routes and Distances

From San Francisco, Paradise Point Marina is reached by driving east on the most convenient route that intersects Interstate 5. Get on I-5 and proceed north past Stockton for about five miles (or south, past the Lodi turnoff at Route 12, which is approximately the same distance) to Eight Mile Road. Take the exit from I-5 and go west on Eight Mile Road for three miles, then south on Rio Blanco Road to the marina.

Bridge Bay Marina is twelve miles north of Redding on Interstate 5. Just before coming to the high bridge across Lake Shasta, look for the prominently marked exit to Bridge Bay Road. Follow this road to the marina.

Accommodations

Houseboat interiors have much in common with luxurious, oversized house trailers, except that houseboats do not have to conform to highway rules and can be built even wider and larger. Moreover, each boat has a large covered foredeck and afterdeck, which practically doubles the living area.

Enjoying sunshine on houseboat roof

The arrangement of sleeping accommodations varies with different boats. A typical ten sleeper, for example, might have a back "bedroom" with double-deck double bunks providing space for four. This room also typically has a full-sized closet and a built-in chest of drawers. At midship is the kitchen and head (boaters' jargon for the lavatory), side by side on the port, with a set of double-deck single bunks across on the starboard. Forward of these, next to the captain's station, is the dinette on one side and a sofa on the other. The sofa extends to make a third double bunk, while the dinette seating unfolds to sleep two more. All in all, this adds up to ten—a lot of people for a single head, although if everyone is good friends, it can work out. Four or six in a boat is more comfortable, however, and for a single couple, the quarters are palatial. Scale all this down a bit for a six sleeper. Again, a full load of six people may be a bit of a crowd, four is more comfortable, and two have room to spare.

On the big boats the head is the real surprise. It is a full bathroom with tub and shower, sink and counter, and a regular toilet.

Your floating resort has enough of everything to sustain normal operation for four or five days before replenishment is necessary. It carries one hundred gallons of water, gasoline sufficient for about twenty-five hours of continuous operation, and enough propane (for operating the hot water heater, refrigerator, and cabin heater) to last even longer. The toilet works on lake water and discharges into a twenty-five-gallon holding tank. If these liquid supplies run short, they can be replenished, and the holding

Wimpy's Marina is favorite port of call on the Delta

tank discharged, at one of the marinas along the way.

Activities

The main "activity" on a houseboat vacation is operation of the boat. Some people are skilled mariners who need little additional instruction; others have never handled anything bigger than an outboard. In either case, the routine familiarization process is thorough and quickly accomplished.

First you check into the marina and are assigned to a boat, which has been provisioned and readied the evening before, and to a staff member who conducts the shakedown. The staff person carefully goes over a checklist of items that needs to be explained, demonstrating working parts where necessary. Fuel supply, refueling procedures, water, propane, fire extinguishers, oven and refrigerator operation, and bedding and linen storage are described. Then come engine operation and boat handling. On the Delta, tide tables and anchoring procedures also are explained. Docking, beaching, and tying up for the night are demonstrated, and a map and navigational advice are provided. Finally, you select a handful of free tapes to play on the ship's stereo system, and with that are on your own to proceed as fancy dictates.

To boating purists, houseboats seem boxy and ungainly, but they are surprisingly maneuverable for their size, and practically fool-proof to handle after you have had a little practice. When first starting out, a good way to try out new landing techniques is to find an abandoned dock and make a few practice landings, coming up into the current, until you have the feel of it.

These are really party boats, designed specifically to provide comfort and fun, but as the check-out person tactfully will suggest, they are not hotels either; someone has to pay attention to the navigation, the maps, and the tide charts. But this is all part of the fun. Particularly on the Delta, with its labyrinthine system of channels and streams and many false openings, it is necessary to plan a route and calculate arrival times, then look sharply for landmarks and check the clock to keep from wandering off course. To old-timers, this is all automatic and soon becomes so for newcomers. If you nevertheless should suffer the misfortune of getting lost, nothing serious is apt to result; sooner or later you will stumble on another boat or a shoreside marina and will find out where you are.

It doesn't take long either to learn the ropes about beaching on a sandy shore in order for you and the crew to stretch your legs or take a swim. Or the houseboat can be taken in and held just right as you cast bait over to the edge of the floating seaweed beds, under which the largemouth bass lurk. Fishing is rarely dull in either the Delta, which also has black bass, striped bass, catfish, and occasional salmon and sturgeon, or in Lake Shasta, which has even more species. Seventeen varieties of game fish have been reported there.

The roof of a houseboat makes a fine place for sunbathing, and because it is so high, affords the best vantage point from which to sight-see or take photographs of the multitude of water birds that inhabits the Delta. Just remember, there are occasional low bridges and tree branches overhanging the water: *do not ride facing the stern.*

Dining

Part of the fun of houseboating is finding your way to a new restaurant, making a graceful approach to the dock, and tying up for a stint ashore and a good meal. Perhaps there also will be entertainment or at least a chance to rub elbows with fellow mariners, trading experiences and information about things to discover and other places to dine.

The Delta is full of such destinations. The map lists fifty marinas with some kind of restaurant facilities, but cooking aboard is fun, too. Nighttime on the water can be inky black and there is too much danger of running aground or into an obstruction to make night cruising advisable. About an hour before dusk, therefore, houseboaters who are not going to a restaurant start looking for a good place to stop that will be out of the channel and not in the line of nighttime traffic. Abandoned floating docks, which can rise and fall with the tide, are ideal and are plentiful in some parts of the Delta. Otherwise, anchor the boat fore and aft in a place where the water will be deep enough to keep the houseboat afloat during the next low tide.

On Lake Shasta another mooring technique is required: beach the front end of the boat on a secluded shore, drive two iron stakes into the ground or find a couple of trees, and securely tie up the houseboat for the night. Then fire up the barbecue on the foredeck and dinner begins.

Kitchenettes on even the smaller crafts are comparatively roomy and easy to work in. On the ten sleepers, they are almost as convenient as a conventional kitchen. The refrigerator has a freezer compartment and plenty of storage space. There also is an ice chest on the deck. For a long cruise, or if there will be a big crew and lots of food to carry, you can load the chest with block ice and a few bags of cubes to augment the refrigerator space.

The propane stove and oven in the galley take care of everything that cannot be barbecued. All the boats have plenty of cookware, utensils, dinnerware, dish towels, and detergent. The pumps must be turned on when water is needed; otherwise, the kitchen setup is just like the one at home.

Monterey Peninsula, Carmel Valley, and the Big Sur

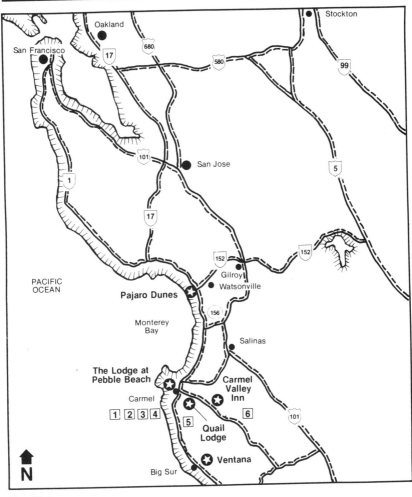

Wayside Inns

1 Pine Inn	3 Stonehouse Guest Lodge	5 Highlands Inn
2 Normandy Inn	4 San Antonio House	6 The Valley Lodge

Pajaro Dunes

Distances:

From San Francisco—87 miles; allow 1½ hours

From Los Angeles—370 miles; allow 7½ hours

Features:

Individual houses, townhouses, and condominiums; remarkable setting among low dunes and cypress groves, all bordering a wide, flat Pacific Ocean beach

Activities:

Walking and jogging along the beach, clam digging, surf-fishing, swimming, surfing, kiteflying, tennis, inspecting architectural extravaganzas, bird-watching; golf nearby

Seasons:

Year around; best weather from September through November.

Rates:

Two-day weekend in one-bedroom condominium—$170 to $180, in two-bedroom townhouse—$320, and in two-bedroom house—$220-$250; all types of accommodations are available with up to four or five bedrooms at correspondingly higher rates; rentals are for a minimum of two nights; weekday rates also are available

Address:

Pajaro Dunes Rental Agency, 2661 Beach Road, Watsonville, California 95076

Phone:

(408) 722-9201

Pajaro Dunes townhouses

One of the most beautiful oceanside communities in California, or anywhere for that matter, Pajaro (pronounced "Pay-ha-ro") Dunes is built on a slender strip of land just one and a half miles long. A shallow tidal slough runs parallel to a stretch of beach along Monterey Bay creating this peninsula, the tip of which is formed by the confluence of the slough and the Pajaro River just before they flow into the sea.

On the ocean side of the peninsula, the golden sand beach is broad and the water shallow for hundreds of feet out into the bay. Windswept cypress trees and low, rolling dunes lie behind the beach, and built into the grassy knolls at rakish angles are some of the wildest, most innovative structures to be found anywhere. This conglomerate of buildings, including houses, townhouses, and condominiums, is just a stone's throw from the beach. A wooden boardwalk runs through the area, joining the various clusters of dwellings.

Forming the border on the east side of this precious strip of real estate, the gently moving slough separates the peninsula from acres and acres of artichokes that grow on the other side of the slough. This sea of green to the east seems almost as vast as the broad ocean vista to the west.

It is hard to believe that as recently as the early 1960s this band of coastland was desolate. Various grandiose schemes for its use had been tried: a racetrack, a tourist camp, hotels, and a dance hall (which was the scene of wild parties in the Roaring Twenties). They came and then disappeared through the years. The only remnant of all this activity was a hardy stand of Holland dune grass, planted in the twenties to stabilize the shifting sands.

Such was the situation in the early 1960s when a farsighted Palo Alto developer envisioned a second-home community along this beach and bought the property, just a few miles from Watsonville. Lots were sold and houses were built in a random pattern among the dunes. Early in the 1970s a big condominium complex was built at Pelican Point, the southern extremity of the property, where the river joins the sea. Later in that decade construction was completed on a cluster of townhouses and another condominium group, the Shore Bird, at the northern end of the property. The development of Pajaro Dunes is now finally complete with 565 units, privately owned and mostly maintained in a year-round rental pool available to those who want to enjoy a seaside vacation.

Routes and Distances

Pajaro Dunes is approximately at the center of the crescent formed by Monterey Bay. To get there from the San Francisco Bay area, drive south on U.S. 101 to Gilroy, twenty-six miles south of San Jose. At Gilroy, turn west on Route 152 to Watsonville where it joins Highway 129. Go through Watsonville on 129 until it terminates at a junction with Highway 1. Cross Highway 1 via an underpass (this is the Riverside exit) and go immediately right to West Beach Road, then left on Beach Road. Signs will point to Sunset State Beach. Continue straight to the beach, where the Pajaro Dunes gatehouse will be on the left. The rental office is just inside the gate.

Approaching from the north or south on Highway 1, take the Riverside exit (look for a big Chevron station on the west side), then follow the instructions given above.

Accommodations

As previously mentioned, most of the 565 units in the Pajaro Dunes complex are in the rental pool. Clustered in groups along the beach, they enjoy maximum protection because they can be reached only by passing through a security-guard station.

The three basic types of rentals are individual homes, a small group of townhouses, and two large condominium complexes. On the extreme ends of the peninsula are the two condominium groups, the most likely choices for couples because they have more single-bedroom units. The houses and townhouses, built along the dunes between the two condominium complexes, each have a minimum of two bedrooms, and generally are rented to families or other groups.

Bird watchers should make a point of staying in the Pelican Point condominiums where, in addition to an ocean view, they will have a

Over two hundred varieties of birds are found around Pajaro Dunes

perfect vantage point from which to watch the waterfowl around the mouth of the Pajaro River. The Shore Bird complex, at the southern end of the property, is built on the dunes and is closer to the beach.

Since all of the accommodations at Pajaro Dunes are individually owned, they are decorated in a variety of ways; some are quite elegant and others are beachy and imaginative, but all are tasteful and comfortable. All of the units have modern kitchens, most of which have a double oven and a dishwasher. Most units also have a washer and dryer. In addition, each unit has a fireplace with an abundant supply of wood, a barbecue on the deck, television, and a stereo music system. You will feel even more spoiled when you find a San Francisco newspaper on your doorstep to enjoy with your morning coffee.

The individual houses offer the most variety. The exterior forms vary from low-slung cottages to three-story houses on stilts. Having two to five bedrooms, they come in every size and shape, including a castle, a windmill, and a pagoda, all of which fit harmoniously into the scene.

The newest and most elegant units are the townhouses. Built on several levels, they are well decorated and spacious and have two to five bedrooms, each with its own bath. Most houses have two decks off the living area, one with a panoramic ocean view and the other with an orientation to the tennis courts. These townhouses work out exceptionally well for house parties or family reunions because of the large common

Surf-casting is common activity at Pajaro Dunes

space in the living-dining area and the privacy of the bedroom-bath suites. They also are excellent for tennis groups because the courts in this area are available on a first-come first-served basis and it is easy to set up group play.

It should be pointed out that all rentals at Pajaro Dunes are for a minimum of two nights and there are no seasonal variations in the rates.

Activities

Inasmuch as Pajaro Dunes is right at the ocean's edge, it is no surprise that a great many of the resort's activities center around the broad sandy beach. The long shallow gradient of this particular stretch of beach makes the area ideal for swimming in the surf, floating on air mattresses, and learning how to surf. However, caution and good judgment must be exercised, as is always the case in the ocean, because of the dangers of riptides and undertows.

An even more popular activity is strolling along the beach, enjoying the salt air and watching a fascinating array of birds that appear to be trying to make a living at the surf's edge. Sandpipers, sanderlings, and a wide variety of what are locally known as "L.B.Js" (little brown jobs) busily follow the waves in and out, pecking at unseen objects in the sand, while gulls circle above. Over two hundred varieties of birds are seen in the area, many of them in the marshy fields on Pelican Point at the confluence

Unusual architecture abounds at Pajaro Dunes

of the slough and the river. Snowy egrets, pelicans, and California quail are but a few of the interesting varieties to look for.

Joggers and fishermen surf-casting for perch along the water's edge are common sights at Pajaro Dunes and, during the clamming season, diggers can be spotted up and down the beach with their clam guns and buckets. The updrafts caused by the dunes provide prime conditions for kiteflying, which has become a favorite hobby on the beach. The resort's rental office has a variety of kites for sale for those guests who would like to try the sport.

A stroll along the beach can be extended onto the boardwalk among the dunes to check out the dramatic architecture of the beach houses. Another way to explore is to take a bicycle along the community's winding asphalt roads. Bikes are available in the rental office. They are so popular for getting about that cars are infrequently seen on the community roadways.

Off the beach, the primary activity at Pajaro Dunes is tennis, played on nineteen courts that are scattered throughout the resort. There are two main tennis centers, each of which has a pro shop, one at the northern end and one at the southern end of the property, with another two courts between the townhouses. All of the courts are carefully located and fenced for wind protection so that playing conditions are excellent most of the time. In the open fields near the tennis centers, volleyball, baseball, touch football, and other recreational programs for children often are organized.

Golfers need to go but a short distance to find good courses. Within a few minutes of the Dunes is the Pajaro Valley Country Club, and in the nearby Santa Cruz area are several others, including the Pasatiempo Golf Course. And less than an hour away are the world famous Monterey Peninsula courses, Pebble Beach and Spyglass Hill.

If you have time for sight-seeing, areas around the Dunes have many interesting sights and activities, only a few of which we can describe here. After just a twenty-minute drive north, you can be in the pretty little town of Santa Cruz, enjoying its famous boardwalk and amusement park. Traveling slightly farther north, you can climb aboard an 1890 steam train at Roaring Camp for an excursion into the Santa Cruz Mountains and redwood forests. Traveling south to the Monterey area, you can explore picturesque Cannery Row, celebrated in the literature of John Steinbeck, or perhaps take the Seventeen Mile Drive to see the sights along the famous coastline of the Monterey Peninsula.

Dining

It is possible that dining in at the Dunes can be more fun than going out, when you consider the fully equipped kitchens and lovely dining areas found in these accommodations. In addition, the large decks off the living areas provide panoramic ocean views for eating outside in fair weather.

If, however, you prefer to go out, there are innumerable good places in both directions along the coast, with both Santa Cruz to the north and Carmel to the south being quite close. The resort's rental office maintains a complete list, with directions for getting there, of all the restaurants within driving range. We will mention just a few of the possibilities. A Mexican restaurant, The Rancho Grande in nearby Watsonville, has an informal atmosphere and authentic, bountiful, and moderately priced food. The Cafe Rio, just twelve minutes north of the Dunes at Rio Del Mar in the Santa Cruz area, is a small restaurant with a bustling atmosphere and a reputation for fine seafood. Trout is the house specialty, but the shellfish also can be highly recommended.

Perhaps the most unusual and well-known restaurant in the area is Shadowbrook at Capitola, also on the way to Santa Cruz. A favorite with natives and visitors alike, Shadowbrook is an excellent steak and seafood house built in an old mansion overlooking the Santa Cruz River. It is reached by descending a steep hill in an outdoor elevator that lands in a beautifully landscaped and flood-lighted garden. Dinner is served in the many nooks and crannies of the old house, with dim lighting allowing a splendid view of the river and garden. One of the most fascinating aspects of the interior decor is an invasion of ivy that has grown through from the outer facade and now festoons the inside walls.

The Lodge
At Pebble Beach

Distances:

From San Francisco—120 miles; allow 2½ hours

From Los Angeles—337 miles; allow 7 hours

Features:

A big, elegant resort with moderate climate year around; Pebble Beach is known world-wide as the site of the annual Bing Crosby Pro-Am Golf Tournament; the beautiful golf course skirts Carmel Bay, and the lodge and housing units overlook both the course and the bay

Activities:

Golf, tennis, horseback riding, hiking, swimming, deep-sea sport fishing, shopping and sight-seeing throughout the surrounding area

Seasons:

Year around; best weather from September through November; spring is lovely; summer tends to be foggy; slowest months are December and January

Rates:

$125 to $135 for two people, plus eight percent room tax

Address:

Pebble Beach, California 93953

Phone:

(408) 624-3811

The Lodge at Pebble Beach

Internationally renowned, the Lodge at Pebble Beach is truly the most distinctive resort on the central California seacoast. Located along the famous Seventeen Mile Drive, it is perched on a low bluff surrounded on three sides by water and facing the white sand beaches of Carmel and the Santa Lucia Mountains in the distance. This section of coastline, well known for its rolling surf, rugged rock formations, and gnarled cypress trees twisted into weird shapes by the wind, is a veritable paradise for the artist and photographer.

The original lodge, a rambling log structure, was built in 1909 to serve as a way station for guests staying at Monterey's palatial Del Monte Hotel, at that time one of the finest hotels in America and a playground for the wealthy. A prime interest of the guests was to take carriage excursions along the scenic Seventeen Mile Drive, which skirts the water's edge of the Monterey Peninsula, stopping at the rustic lodge to dine and rest. The visitors loved the big, informal lobby with a fireplace so large, the story goes, that it took two men and a truck to fill it with logs for an evening's blaze. Many guests came to prefer it to the elegant and formal old hotel, and a few years later, when a row of cottages was added for overnight guests, it became popular as a weekend resort.

As has been the fate of so many wood-framed hostelries, the old lodge burned to the ground in 1917. In its place a structure with broad terraces was erected, and between the new lodge and the ocean a spectacular golf course was laid out that was destined to become the most celebrated in California. Today, in fact, it is regarded by experts as one of the five finest courses in the world.

The new lodge, while retaining its informal hospitality, became the most fashionable hostelry in the area and was highly touted, as it still is, for its fine accommodations, excellent service, and outstanding cuisine. In the meantime, Del Monte Properties, owner of the lodge and the seven thousand surrounding acres, sold large residential parcels bordering the golf course and the Seventeen Mile Drive; the area since has become one of the most prestigious residential areas in California. Recreational facilities of all kinds—three golf courses, tennis courts, a beach club, and an equestrian center—were developed for the pleasure of the residents and the guests of the lodge.

In addition to having these features, Pebble Beach is in the heart of Del Monte Forest and close to the charming little town of Carmel, fascinating Cannery Row in Monterey, the Big Sur country, and many other points of interest. The climate, which is beautiful and moderate year around, enhances the pursuit of all these activities. With the exception of a few foggy periods, particularly during the summer months, the weather is quite reliable. Fall is the most beautiful season, and it is not uncommon to see guests celebrating the Thanksgiving holiday in their bathing suits.

Distinctive pines mark Pebble Beach grounds

Routes and Distances

After passing Monterey heading south on Highway 1, look for a right-hand turnoff to Pebble Beach. Signs will direct you to the road to the lodge, which is also the start of the well-known Seventeen Mile Drive, where you will encounter a gatehouse with security guards. If you have a confirmed reservation at the lodge, they promptly will let you through. Otherwise, you will pay a small toll, which later will be reimbursed when you register. The lodge is approximately two miles from the gatehouse.

Accommodations

Only a dozen of the approximately 150 guest rooms at Pebble Beach are in the lodge itself. The others are in twelve attractive two-story buildings, some of which take advantage of the view across the final hole of the golf course, while others enjoy a more panoramic view on a hillside above the lodge.

In accordance with the management's high standards, an ongoing remodeling and refurbishing program ensures fresh and attractive appointments in every room, using a tasteful country French decor, and providing many other niceties intended to make your stay as pleasant as possible. Most of the units have fireplaces, with a fire laid in the hearth and a basket of extra wood there when you arrive. In a typical unit, two big wing-back chairs, with an antique lamp table between them, face the fireplace and make a cozy sitting area. The arrangement also faces an

The famous seventh hole at Pebble Beach

alcove with a television in the wall above a bar and a small refrigerator. Each unit also has two elegant queen-sized beds, and a dressing room with a large closet, a sink, and a three-way mirror. The bathroom has another sink, a combination bath and shower, and even a telephone. All of the lower level units have sliding glass doors and a private patio, while the upper units have individual balconies.

Returning from dinner you will find that the maid has turned down your bed, and when you awake, the morning newspaper will be on your doorstep. Hoping your stay will be so pleasant that you will be reluctant to leave, the management allows a 2:00 P.M. check-out. Small, well-behaved pets also are allowed if they are kept on leashes.

Activities

Golf reigns supreme at Pebble Beach, even though there are numerous other activities in which to participate. Since this is one of the most renowned and challenging courses in the world, people come from distant lands for the express purpose of testing themselves against its difficulties. It is only one of three outstanding courses in the immediate area, however. There is also Spyglass Hill, which was beautifully laid out by the famous golfer Robert Trent Jones, and the Old Del Monte course, which is reputed to be the oldest links in California and possibly west of the Mississippi. When really big tournaments such as the Bing Crosby Pro-Amateur are held in the area, it is a distinct advantage to have this complex

Beach and Tennis Club pool at Pebble Beach

of courses to handle the field.

When staying at the lodge, no real golf buff would ever be satisfied if he or she did not try the giant killer, Pebble Beach, although on subsequent rounds the less difficult Spyglass Hill or Old Del Monte might look pretty inviting. Even when played from the regular tees, Pebble Beach is a hard 6,389 yards of rolling terrain, closely hugging the rocky Pacific coastline.

The greens fee at Pebble Beach is considerably higher than at the other courses, but it includes the use of an electric cart, which is mandatory. The fee at Spyglass Hill, where carts are optional, is just about half as much, with Old Del Monte slightly less than that.

Guests staying at Pebble Beach are granted full privileges for use of the Beach and Tennis Club, where there are thirteen championship tennis courts, two paddle tennis courts, a fully equipped pro shop, and a tennis professional available for private lessons. (An hourly fee is charged for use of the courts.) The club also has an outdoor, Olympic-sized, freshwater pool that features a magnificent view of Carmel Bay from its deck, and also provides dressing rooms and saunas for the convenience of the guests. For those who prefer sunning at the water's edge, there is a small sandy beach right below the clubhouse.

Just a short distance from the lodge is the Equestrian Center. On horseback you can ride over thirty-four miles of trails that lead through the heart of the heavily wooded Del Monte Forest up to higher terrain and superb views of the Pacific coastline. Hikers also are welcome to explore these trails, and the staff at the lodge is happy to pack picnic lunches for a day's outing.

For joggers, a par course has been laid out just across the road from the lodge. However, many joggers who are up early enough to beat the golfers out on the course prefer running along the cart paths leading from hole to hole. The added bonuses are the bracing salt air that drifts in off Carmel Bay and the magnificent views.

Deep-sea sport fishing is another popular activity on the peninsula, with charter boats leaving every day from the Monterey Marina. Just ask at the transportation desk in the lodge for help in making arrangements for a trip.

A more sedentary but always popular activity at Pebble Beach is strolling along the shopping lane across from the lodge. Everything from fine clothing, jewelry, and luggage to flowers, wine, and delicatessen fare are included in this interesting arcade of shops, and lazily poking around in them is a pleasant respite from a strenuous day of golf or tennis.

Dining

It is not surprising that many people who are not guests of the lodge make a point of stopping by while touring the Seventeen Mile Drive, because there are a number of excellent places to eat at Pebble Beach.

The Cypress Room is the original grand dining room at the lodge, with a view overlooking the eighteenth hole of the golf course, the water, and the mountains in the distance. The beautiful table settings, crystal, and giant chandeliers, as well as the attentive service of a very professional staff, create an atmosphere of formal elegance. The fine continental cuisine features a variety of meat and fish entrées, with the veal piccata and the sautéed prawns being especially memorable. And as would be expected, there is an exceptional selection of both French and domestic wines. Dinner dancing to live music is a special weekend feature in the Cypress Room on Friday, Saturday, and Sunday evenings beginning at eight. Jackets are required for dinner, but sports attire is very acceptable for breakfast and lunch, which are served here daily.

For another adventure in formal dining, you can go downstairs to the Club XIX, a small French restaurant where dinner is served by candlelight in an intimate atmosphere and delectable dishes such as abalone from Monterey Bay, Chateaubriand, and a variety of veal dishes are cooked to perfection. Luncheon also is served here. And on nice days, there are cocktails on the terrace lounge, which opens off the restaurant and makes an excellent vantage point from which to watch golfers putting out the final hole of the course.

The golfers themselves are apt to retire to a third place, the Tap Room, when they come off the course because they are welcome there in their golfing attire and feel at home for an informal drink or lunch amid walls lined with old photographs of past tournaments and famous foursomes, as well as other golfing memorabilia.

Finally, as a guest at the lodge you also have membership privileges at the Beach and Tennis Club, a quarter mile away, which has its own pleasant dining room—an especially nice place for lunch, or for its very special Sunday brunch.

Off premises, in Carmel and Monterey, there are dozens of other restaurants, many of which are listed in the Quail Lodge and Carmel Valley Inn chapters. If you do not want to go out at all, however, the lodge is famous for its room service. All meals, breakfast through dinner, are available, and at reasonable prices. It should be noted that at the time of the final bill, a service charge is added to cover all extras such as room service, sparing guests the nuisance of tipping during their vacation.

Quail Lodge

Distances:

From San Francisco—128 miles; allow 2¾ hours

From Los Angeles—343 miles; allow 7½ hours

Features:

Quintessential good taste and good management; a beautiful, quiet, relaxed garden setting in Carmel Valley; only five minutes from the ocean, but far enough away to escape the fog and enjoy good weather for outdoor sports

Activities:

Golf, tennis, swimming, "hot tubbing" on premises; ocean beaches at nearby Carmel; shopping and sight-seeing on Monterey Peninsula; exploring the Seventeen Mile Drive and the Big Sur coastline

Seasons:

Year around

Rates:

$120 to $138 for two people

Address:

8205 Valley Greens Drive, Carmel, California 93923

Phone:

(408) 624-1581

Covey Restaurant at Quail Lodge

In 1980 Quail Lodge was one of only eight hotels in the United States to receive the Mobil Travel Guide's coveted five-star award. It was well deserved. Few places offer the combination of quiet, privacy, elegance, and beauty that Quail Lodge affords its guests.

The main lodge building is impressive, with soaring lines and a sweeping roof, partially cantilevered over a blue lagoon populated by colorful water birds. Spread out on either side of the lodge, and separated from each other by the lagoon and putting greens and a swimming pool, are fifteen separate buildings containing the rooming accommodations. Facing these are the tree-lined, lake-dotted fairways of the Carmel Valley Golf and Country Club, with a picturesque stream meandering its length.

Carmel Valley is famous for its generally good weather. The heavy fog that often accumulates along the coast, dissipates rapidly a short way into the valley, and the temperature rises accordingly. Quail Lodge and the country club deliberately were located to be close to the Monterey Peninsula, while still taking full advantage of the valley's fine weather. Although the lodge and the country club are separate entities, they occupy the same 245-acre site and lodge guests, who have full country club privileges, think of them as one. Between the lodge and the club there are two restaurants and two lounges, and across the entrance road from the lodge is another restaurant and a group of country stores, where incidental items may be purchased.

A dozen varieties of ducks populate Quail Lodge lagoon

Fine weather, top-notch sports facilities, and excellent dining, in addition to an uncommon supply of charm and comfort, mark Quail Lodge as the kind of getaway you come to when you are happy to stay put. There is no end of other attractions in the vicinity, to be sure, but they hardly will be missed if you just want to remain on the premises.

Routes and Distances

Quail Lodge is easy to find. From the north, skirt Monterey Bay on Highway 1, passing Seaside and the town of Monterey. Just beyond the turnoff to Carmel, you will encounter a well-marked junction with County Road G16, which leads to Carmel Valley. Take this road east for approximately five minutes, then begin looking for the Quail Lodge sign on the right. The lodge is just a few yards off the main road.

From the south, come all the way on Highway 1 and turn just before Carmel on G16 as instructed above, or take U.S. 101 north to Salinas and from there Route 68 west to Monterey and the intersection with the coastal highway, then south again to G16.

Accommodations

Quail Lodge's accommodations are characterized by a lot of space, furniture, and good taste. A typical room has a king-sized bed, dresser,

Lush grounds at Quail Lodge

end tables, a game table with four armchairs, a writing desk and chair, and a lounge chair or chairs, all scattered with room to spare. Outside, in a little private patio (or in some cases, a deck), is your own garden furniture. A dressing room, which is screened from the living area, has a closet, a wide counter, a lavatory, and a separate bath. On the counter you will find a percolator with a supply of freshly ground coffee, plus packets of cream and sugar, instant Sanka, and cocoa. (Upon arrival, you also will be greeted with a split of champagne as a welcoming gift from the manager— a little touch that illustrates the lodge's taste for gracious details.)

Most of the rooms or suites, which are arranged in groups of five, are at ground level in low-lying cottages designed so that each unit has a private entrance and a patio well screened with plantings. The central unit in each group is slightly larger than the others and has a fireplace and wet bar, so it has a higher rate. Because there are connecting doors between each of the five units, they can be converted into suites of two, three, or four bedrooms, using the central section as a common living room.

Besides the low cottages there also are a few two-story buildings with balcony rooms, which have decks instead of patios. The decks provide views of the golf course and the hills that surround the valley. Some of these upper rooms also have fireplaces, which, if desired, should be requested specifically upon making reservations.

Activities

Summers in Carmel Valley are usually warm, spring and fall are always delightful, and winters are mild. The many fine sunny days in November and December make tennis and lounging by the swimming pool pleasant; tennis is often possible even in January and February.

Golf, however, is the major sport here and can be played the year around. The whole Monterey area, of course, is famous for its golf courses (see the "Activities" section of The Lodge at Pebble Beach chapter), with many of them nationally known and some highly respected for their difficulty. The one at the Carmel Valley Golf and Country Club has many water hazards, and is handsomely maintained. Of average difficulty, it has a par of seventy-one and a 69.8 rating. The total length for its eighteen holes is 6,175 yards.

The clubhouse for the country club is about a quarter mile from the lodge. You can drive around to it or walk along the cart trail paralleling the fourteenth fairway. On the ground floor of the clubhouse is a large, well-equipped pro shop for both golf and tennis supplies. A driving range is just outside, and across the street, behind shrubbery windbreaks, are four hard-surfaced tennis courts. The upper level of the clubhouse has a restaurant and bar, while alongside in a courtyard is a swimming pool. Everything can be used by lodge guests, although moderate fees are charged for use of the courts and greens.

The lodge's own swimming pool lies in a sun pocket behind thick shrubbery close to the rooms. This is the favorite place for swimming and lounging. The water is always kept pleasantly warm. On a deck under an open-air gazebo above the pool is a large wooden hot tub with water at the ideal temperature of 104 degrees.

Away from the lodge, for anyone who wants a change of pace, there are all the shopping and exploring opportunities around Monterey Peninsula and along the Big Sur coast, as mentioned in the chapter on Carmel Valley Inn. Another place to visit, just a few minutes distant, near the Highway 1 junction, is The Barnyard, an improbable shopping mall made up of nine strangely shaped, authentic old barns, all connected with walkways and garden paths and filled with dozens of shops and galleries and restaurants with outdoor dining areas. It requires several hours to investigate this big complex thoroughly, but the time probably will be considered well spent. To find The Barnyard, look for its symbol, an old-fashioned farm windmill that stands high above the surrounding buildings and can be seen from all directions.

Dining

Quail Lodge's Covey Restaurant is acknowledged to be one of the better dinner houses in the whole Carmel-Monterey area, both for excellence of food preparation and the quiet elegance of its setting. The

Outdoor restaurant in The Barnyard

menu is "continental cuisine," another way of saying it is strongly French in character.

To enter the dining room, one passes a dark intimate bar, with low tables, upholstered couches, and a crackling fire in the fireplace. Inside, the tables are arranged at varying levels in small, sequestered groups, with little individual kerosene lamps providing practically the only light; this all is designed to carry out the feeling of intimacy established by the bar. The interior is dark oak, set off with pewter serving platters at each place and comfortable high-back spool chairs. The view is over the lagoon toward a sparkling fountain, carefully night-lighted for dramatic effect. Before dark, multi-hued ducks swim serenely under the windows.

The Covey is obviously not inexpensive, but is by all means the place to go for the "big night" that highlights your vacation. It is open only for dinner. For breakfast, you walk across the golf course to the clubhouse, where you can enjoy a view, over orange juice and eggs, of golfers teeing off on the first hole or practicing on the driving range. Guests bring their clubs or rackets, and remain all day to play golf or tennis, or to swim in the pool and then have lunch. Should it be preferable, however, to go back to the rooms before lunch, then the little Carousel Garden Restaurant in the group of western-style stores across from the lodge is handily situated. It is informal, attractively appointed inside, and has a pretty outdoor dining area in the garden, from which it takes its name.

After having exhausted the possibilities of the Covey, the Clubhouse, and the Carousel Garden, there is the whole panoply of the peninsula to choose from with as thick a concentration of good restaurants as anywhere on the West Coast. Monterey's Fisherman's Wharf and Cannery Row, for example, both deserve a bit of culinary exploration, and in Carmel, The Fish House on Sixth Street serves good food and is easy to find, just opposite the city park.

Carmel Valley Inn

Distances:

From San Francisco—132 miles; allow 2¾ hours

From Los Angeles—348 miles; allow 7½ hours

Features:

Close-knit facilities and an informal atmosphere; located well back in Carmel Valley, out of the fog zone; generally sunny weather facilitates all outdoor activities

Activities:

Tennis, swimming, "hot tubbing" on premises; golf, horseback riding nearby; shopping and sight-seeing on the Monterey Peninsula, exploring the Big Sur country

Seasons:

Year around

Rates:

$38 to $56 for two people; weekdays are less expensive than weekends

Address:

P.O. Box 115, Carmel Valley, California 93924

Phone:

(408) 659-3131

Entrance to Carmel Valley Inn

Often in the spring and summer when heavy fog drifts in from the ocean to cover Monterey Bay and the beautiful white beaches of Carmel, the weather can be cool and dank. But several miles inland in Carmel Valley, the fog gradually thins until suddenly the warm sunshine appears. The temperature often will be as much as thirty degrees warmer, which is perfect for the easy life-style at Carmel Valley Inn, where most of the time will be spent outdoors.

The climate, the character of the land, and the density of population in Carmel Valley are radically different from those of the Monterey Peninsula, yet the latter, with its many attractions, is never more than twenty minutes away. The valley itself is the legendary place where "Mack and the boys" hunted for the frogs they used for currency in John Steinbeck's book *Cannery Row*. The valley's narrow floor is still lush with growth, and undoubtedly still full of frogs, in contrast to the dry, sparsely timbered foothills of the bordering Santa Lucia Mountains.

The arrangement of the inn takes advantage of the climate and terrain in a way that makes outdoor living easy. Billing itself as "your own private tennis resort," its seven courts are available at no extra charge to guests and are located close to the accommodations so that it is convenient to step out and see at a glance whether a court is available.

Inside the square formed by the buildings is a large, solar-heated swimming pool, and next to that, off the bar, is an outdoor dining terrace.

Furnished to resemble a European sidewalk café, this is the natural focal point of the inn where guests drift back after their activities to relax and make friends, or just enjoy the glorious valley sunshine.

Routes and Distances

California's Highway 1 closely follows the contours of Monterey Bay. From north or south, follow Route 1 to County Road G16 just south of Carmel. Take this road for approximately eleven miles, then look for Carmel Valley Inn's "running fox" sign on the left.

Accommodations

Reasonable prices are a big attraction at Carmel Valley Inn, where the accommodations are good and comfortable but not fancy. The rooms are in several single-story buildings close to the main building, which contains the lobby, restaurant, and lounge. A typical double room might have a king-sized bed, a small table with two lounge chairs, color television (but no phone), and a bath with a separate dressing area and lavatory. A separate entrance opens directly onto the lawn or, in some buildings, onto a deck.

The lobby is a friendly, cedar-paneled, open-beamed room with a huge fireplace, and most memorable, a five-foot birdcage containing two magnificent white cockatoos, the manager's pride. He takes them home at night and returns them to their cage each morning, to the delight of his guests.

The inn's bar adjoins the lobby, and both areas are filled with lounge furniture and card tables, making them the communal center of the inn whenever guests gather indoors. In one corner, there is a big projection television screen, which can be used for showing movies in the evening or football in the fall. During the football season, special "stadium dinners" are served right in the lobby so nobody has to miss the critical action.

These physical arrangements at Carmel Valley Inn, and the laid-back attitude of the staff, make it easy for guests to slip into the spirit of the place and quickly commence what they have come for: a relaxed good time.

Activities

Tennis is number one here, followed by sunning, swimming, taking jaunts into Carmel and Monterey, and exploring the Big Sur coastline.

To tennis players, the big advantages of the inn are the relatively high courts-to-rooms ratio and the predominantly good weather, which together guarantees lots of playing time. A tennis professional is on hand year around to supervise activities and help those who see their vacation as an opportunity to improve their game. All the courts are hard surfaced, in good condition, and individually fenced.

The inn's pool, sheltered by the first of the hills rising to the east, catches all the long afternoon sun, making poolside lounging and swimming comfortable nine months of the year. In the summer, luncheon and cocktails are served at poolside to take full advantage of this nicely situated facility.

The unusual white sand beach at Carmel, no more than twenty minutes away and a particularly good destination for a picnic, should not be missed if the weather on the coast is good. You will find it right at the foot of Ocean Avenue, the main street of Carmel. Drive straight through town; at the end of the street is a parking lot with a white dune rising above it. Climb the dune and the beach and ocean are spread out below.

Carmel itself is famous for its delightful city planning, which has resulted in an absence of garishness, an abundance of trees, and charming and eclectic architecture. The town is loaded with boutiques, art galleries, and good restaurants, and is small enough that you can park the car and see most of the sights on foot.

On the other side of the peninsula is Monterey, with its famous Fisherman's Wharf, sardine canneries, and many more galleries and shops and other points of interest. Before visiting Monterey check out a copy of John Steinbeck's *Cannery Row* at the library and reread that classic and hilarious description of what this little town on the bay was like before the world discovered it. Steinbeck's story, fresh in your memory, will make your visit remarkably more exciting.

A number of outstanding golf courses are available in the area,

Carmel Valley Inn pool

including Pebble Beach, Spyglass Hill, Cypress Point, and Del Monte. The Carmel Valley Golf and Country Club and Rancho Canada are two more good courses, right in the valley itself and just a few minutes away from the inn.

Carmel Valley runs in a southeasterly direction from Monterey, roughly paralleling the Pacific Ocean. The rugged highlands of the Los Padres National Forest lie between the valley and the ocean. This is striking country and the way to see it is on horseback with a guide who knows where to go. The inn will recommend the Whiffletree Ranch for this purpose. It is eleven miles away, on the edge of the forest, and conducts a variety of rides, including a favorite all-day affair that features fancy food and wine served under the oaks at one of the area's high meadow campsites. The management of the inn will make all the arrangements for this or other riding programs.

Dining

The Monterey area is loaded with good places to eat, making dining out one of the most enjoyable and adventuresome parts of vacationing here. And, as good a start as any is to arrange reservations at the inn's own Fox Hill Restaurant, which calls itself "the affordable French restaurant" and does a good job of living up to the billing. The atmosphere is welcoming, with candlelight, dark linens, and old-fashioned serving platters. Wooden captain's chairs with deep wing backs give the room

Diners at Nepenthe enjoy spectacular views of Big Sur

character, and the floor-to-ceiling windows look out to the Santa Lucia Mountains across the valley. The French cooking includes many flaming dishes prepared at the tables. Hot spinach salad is the house specialty, and typical entrées include apricot duckling and sole amandine. With all dinners a small dish of sherbet and a frosted fork are provided for clearing the palate between courses.

There are literally dozens of other outstanding restaurants in the area. For a night of elegance, for example, go up the valley to the Covey Room at Quail Lodge or the Cypress Room at Pebble Beach (see the "Dining" sections of those two chapters). For atmosphere, drive into Monterey to The Cannery or Steinbeck's Lobster Grotto on Cannery Row. For other suggestions ask the management at the inn what places currently are commanding the most attention.

Luncheon is available around the pool or in the courtyard, so it is not necessary to leave the premises, but it also is fun to drive into Monterey and take a stroll down Fisherman's Wharf. You can lunch at one of the restaurants there or have a take-out lunch from one of the booths that sells seafood tidbits with chips and beer.

The most dramatic experience is to drive down the coast past Big Sur for lunch at Nepenthe or Ventana. The drive along this ruggedly beautiful coastline is exciting and affords glimpses through the trees of fabulous houses that cling to cliffs high above the water's edge or sit on promontories that jut far out into the surf. Big Sur is twenty-nine miles from Carmel. Ventana, in the hills to the east, and Nepenthe, to the west, are a few miles beyond. Both of these places feature outdoor dining in high settings, with breathtaking views over the ocean and down the coast toward San Simeon. Nepenthe is an informal, almost funky restaurant, but great fun. Its menu offers all the regular fare, but a favorite is platters of cheeses and fruits with a carafe of wine, a delightful meal indeed while sitting on a bench under eucalyptus trees trying to see a hundred miles down the coast. Ventana is more conventional, but affords equally exciting views from its broad deck under vine-covered trellises.

Ventana

Distances:

From San Francisco—150 miles; allow 3 hours

From Los Angeles—350 miles; allow 7 hours

Features:

Isolated high in the hills of California's spectacular Big Sur, with Olympian views; a place truly to get away from it all in elegant comfort

Activities:

Swimming in outdoor pool (heated all year), soaking in expansive outdoor spa, taking sauna baths, walking in the hills; contemplation and rest

Seasons:

Year around

Rates:

$125 to $150 for two people in room; $250 for two people in suite; prices include breakfast

Address:

Big Sur, California 93920

Phone:

(408) 667-2331 or (408) 624-4812

Latticework facades characterize Ventana

In writing *The Getaway Guide* series, we have visited resorts so remote as to be accessible only by plane, by boat, or on skis. Now Ventana must be included in this select group because, even though it can be reached by car, the sense of isolation is as strong as at any of the others. In fact, the whole stretch of the Big Sur seems isolated because of its distance from cities and the lack of commercial activity, or even agriculture. Strangers looking for a town can drive right through Big Sur and wonder afterward how they missed it. But that is because it is really just a strip of coast without any focal point or definite borders.

Occupying a commanding hillside back of this stretch of coast, Ventana looks out into the broad Pacific in a way that makes the inn seem even more isolated from the world of busy people. The setting is incredibly lovely, with the residence buildings sitting atop a narrow knoll between steep canyons. The restaurant sits on a neighboring knoll, where it appears quite close but actually is a quarter mile away by the road, which snakes down into the valley and up the other side. In this country the tops of the knolls are bare meadowland, but the canyons unexpectedly are filled with giant trees so that the inn's rooms on the canyon edge look out into a forest of redwoods and gnarled oaks.

Spanish for "window," the name Ventana was chosen because this location is like a window opening to the Pacific on one side and the hidden forest on the other. In another sense, however, windows serve a different

Oaks in canyon shelter Ventana buildings

function: you can see out through them, but sometimes they act as a mirror in which you see yourself reflected. Ventana is thus a place for looking out, but also for turning inward to reflect upon yourself and to contemplate in the serenity of a quiet environment.

Routes and Distances

From San Francisco take U.S. 101 south to Prunedale. At Prunedale, Highway 156 cuts across to intersect Highway 1 on the coast at Castroville. Follow Highway 1 south, past Seaside and Carmel for about twenty-seven miles until you see the markers for Pfeiffer–Big Sur State Park. A mile past the park look for Ventana's sign on the left.

From Carmel Highlands to Big Sur is a remarkable stretch of scenic highway, with many turnoffs and vista points. It is well worthwhile to allow extra time in order to make the most of this drive.

Accommodations

Although Ventana is relatively new (the original buildings went up in 1975), the weathered cedar exteriors make the structures appear much older. The eight two-story buildings scattered on the hillside all have unusual peaked rooflines, like gables cut in half and latticed over to provide shade from the sun. Each building has six units, all with private decks overlooking either the ocean or a wooded ravine with mountains in the background. Numerous black crows in the giant trees in the ravine occasionally carry on raucous conversations, breaking the otherwise perfect solitude.

All forty rooms at Ventana are unusually spacious, especially those on the second level, which have lofted ceilings reaching about eighteen feet at the highest point. Two of the interior walls are finished in a rough golden cedar paneling, and cedar louvers provide light control and privacy on the window walls. All but a few units have big Franklin stoves set on raised tile hearths, along with generous supplies of wood. A large dressing room and bath complete the makeup of each unit (with the exception of a few very elegant, even more spacious two-room suites).

The interior design at Ventana will please the most discriminating guest. One example is the careful attention paid to color: those rooms flooded with morning sun are all decorated in gold, while the ones getting afternoon sunshine are done in a cool blue. The large headboard in each unit is hand painted with a unique design, and the lovely patchwork quilt that covers the bed is handmade in Nova Scotia. The furniture is made of either wicker or bamboo and the chairs have bright cushions matching the upholstery of the cozy window seat. Attractive basket lamps hang on long chains over the bed, making nighttime reading a comfortable affair.

Guests begin to get an inkling that they are going to be pampered when they arrive and find an array of fresh flowers in their room, "his" and "hers" freshly laundered kimonos and slippers waiting to be worn to

Ventana pool is protected from wind

the spa, and other thoughtful niceties. They will be certain of it when the maid arrives in the evening to turn down the bed and leave chocolate mints on the nightstand.

Activities

Explicitly designed for rest and relaxation, Ventana is unburdened by a necessity to promote organized activities. Everything about the place invites getting up late, taking it easy, dreaming, and reading. One result is that you see a lot of books at Ventana. People read as they eat breakfast on the deck in the sun or as they lie next to the pool; they even read in the spa and in the private cubicles around it. If you are not in the mood for reading, it is fascinating just to sit and look out over the ocean below, or up at the rim of the hills cradling Ventana.

In the case of the hills, it is difficult to look for long, however, without wondering what is on top and what the views might be like from those heights. More often than not, this kind of contemplation leads to physical exercise. In consideration of the good dinners in store at the inn's restaurant, an appetite-building walk during the afternoon is not a bad idea. The way into the hills is to follow the natural crest of the knoll toward the row of tanks forming the inn's waterworks. At the tanks, follow the little-used gravel road, which makes good walking, except that it is constantly uphill. This road quickly takes you into a remarkable redwood forest, remarkable not only because these great trees are

Pfeiffer–Big Sur State Park near Ventana

unexpected in an area known only for scrub oak, but also because the redwoods are able to grow on the nearly vertical canyon slopes. You find yourself looking directly into the tops of 150-foot trees as you follow the road. At the end of the forested section is a lovely waterfall flowing over a rock between two big trees. From the waterfall the road follows the hill contours, with Ventana only a speck below and the Pacific Ocean beyond. Walk as many miles as you like on this road, as it goes as far into the hills as anyone could want to go.

Pfeiffer–Big Sur State Park also is full of good trails. A beautiful "hidden" beach (its entrance is unmarked, so not many know about it) is a part of this park system. It has good sand, good surf, and great jagged rocks to climb on. Find it by driving north from Ventana about a mile until you pass a bridge, then take the first left down Sycamore Canyon for two miles to the beach. It is a delightful spot to picnic.

After doing the hills or the beach, it is time for the spa. Ventana's is the biggest and most inviting spa we have seen, cleverly designed for direct access from both the men's and women's dressing rooms, but still located outdoors under big oak trees. Baffles divide it into three parts, one for men, one for ladies, and a common portion in the middle. After the spa, step directly into the saunas, again divided into three baffled but connected parts, and after that perhaps take a final refreshing dip in the outdoor pool, which is heated year around. After that you will be ready for more reading and dreaming.

Dining

The day begins at Ventana with the serious decision of where to have breakfast. But while thinking about it, you first can brew a pot of coffee right in your room, as all the equipment is provided, and enjoy the morning paper, which will be found on your doorstep.

On a nice day, nothing is more delightful than breakfasting on your deck, and if this should be your choice, simply call the office and a colorful tray of fresh fruit juice, melon slices, and a variety of pastries will promptly be delivered to your door. In brisk weather, you might prefer to have your tray at the small round table before an open fire in the Franklin stove. Or if you are in a gregarious mood, you can join other guests for the same breakfast in the lounge.

At lunchtime, the scene shifts to the Ventana restaurant on the next knoll. It commands a breathtaking view of the ocean from an immense patio area where luncheon and cocktails are served year around when the weather permits, which fortunately is most of the time. From this terrace on clear days you might not be able to see forever, but it is a fact that you can see sixty miles in one direction and forty in the other. Bright flower beds and trees in planters divide the area, and a trellis arrangement over one section provides filtered sunlight and partial shade on warm days.

Ventana dining terrace overlooks Pacific Ocean

Beautiful Monarch butterflies and many kinds of birds flutter among the trees and lush vines on the trellis. The birds are so friendly they often join guests at their tables to purloin a stray crumb or two. The lunch menu features tasty sandwiches, salads, and spicy omelets.

Just a short distance away on the road to the south is another Big Sur restaurant that should not be missed. This is Nepenthe, which also features outdoor dining with magnificent ocean views. People drive out here for lunch from Carmel and the valley as it is a perfect turn-around point when taking a scenic tour along Big Sur. Sitting on Nepenthe's patio enjoying a sandwich or a fruit and cheese board with a glass of Chablis is pure delight.

An alternative to having lunch at these restaurants is to have a basket packed at the Ventana Deli, then go to the beach or the hills behind the inn for a picnic.

Dinners at Ventana are always a pleasant occasion. The interior of the restaurant is purposely understated to project attention to the ocean and the evening sunsets. Rich wood paneling, an open fireplace, and tall candles on each table create a warm setting, while after dark a flood-lighted patio provides an interesting view from the picture windows running along the ocean side. The excellent food is enhanced by the careful attention the staff gives in preparing it just the way you like it. The menu includes a nice balance of seafood, meat, and fowl, and an extensive wine list.

Pine Inn

Distance: 121 miles from San Francisco, in Carmel, on Ocean Avenue
Features: A very big wayside inn; beautifully appointed; in the very center of
California's most visited village
Rates: $43 to $79 for two people
Address: P.O. Box 250, Carmel, California 93921
Phone: (408) 624-3851

One of Carmel's best-known and most solidly established institutions, the Pine Inn is difficult to characterize. Centrally located on Carmel's busy main street, it is a cross between a large, efficiently managed, elegant city hotel and a small country inn. The ground floor is a maze of shop-lined arcades and awning-covered walkways, complemented by potted trees and wrought iron railings. The inn has four dining rooms and the Red Parlor bar. The two smaller dining rooms are reserved for private parties, while the others, the Garden Room and the Gazeboé, are widely popular both with inn guests and the general public. The Gazeboé is a unique indoor-outdoor room with a roof that rolls back to reveal the sky in good weather. The small-inn effect is created by the Victorian decor—brass bedsteads and flowery wallpaper, shuttered windows in the rooms, and ornate chandeliers. For people who want to "do" Carmel, this is a fine place to start. Reservations made well in advance are advisable.

Normandy Inn

Distance: 121 miles from San Francisco, in Carmel, on Ocean Avenue
Features: A charming French country inn in downtown Carmel; only two blocks from the beach
Rates: $48 to $103 for two people
Address: Box 1706, Carmel, California 93921
Phone: (408) 624-3825

In spite of being right in the middle of town with all the activity that implies, the Normandy Inn has a quiet country flavor. Perhaps this is because it is built around, and the rooms open onto, a flagstone-paved courtyard full of trees and plantings and potted flowers, out of sight of the town. Perhaps it also is due to the authentic French architecture and country furnishings used so effectively throughout.

A wide variety of accommodations is available—everything from just comfortable spacious rooms to rooms with fireplaces, others with kitchens, suites with two rooms, and even some cottages with fireplaces, kitchens, and separate living rooms. Because hardly any two are alike, a conversation with the reservations clerk is advisable in order to suit particular needs. All room rates include a complimentary continental breakfast served buffet style each morning in the inn's colorful country kitchen.

Stonehouse Guest Lodge

Distance: 121 miles from San Francisco, in Carmel, on Eighth, just below Monte Verde
Features: Small, traditionally appointed bed and breakfast house; two blocks from downtown Carmel and four blocks from the beach
Rates: $28 to $34 for two people
Address: P.O. Box 2517, Carmel, California 93921
Phone: (408) 624-4569

Located on a quiet side street, Stonehouse is another good vantage point from which to appreciate Carmel's many charms while avoiding the overcrowding that sometimes occurs. The word "traditional," both in California and New England (few other areas in the United States have such guest houses), is often applied to a turn-of-the-century mansion with big rooms filled with antiques, old-fashioned decorations, and, most important, old-style comfort and hospitality. Stonehouse fits all this to a tee. It has only five guest rooms, but they are charmingly furnished and include fresh flowers and decanters of sherry on the sideboards. All the rooms share two baths "down the hall," as well as the downstairs parlor, where a fire burns cheerfully morning and evening. There is a big ivy-covered front porch and a sun-room where coffee is available, along with color television and backgammon and other games. Continental breakfast is served in the dining room.

San Antonio House

Distance: 121 miles from San Francisco, in Carmel, on San Antonio Avenue, between Ocean Avenue and Seventh, one block from the beach
Features: European-style guest house; out of the mainstream, but nevertheless close to Carmel's many attractions
Rates: $45 to $50 for two people
Address: P.O. Box 3683, Carmel, California 93921
Phone: (408) 624-4334

The nice thing about San Antonio House is its location—a quiet, shady side street where parking is no problem and the bumper-to-bumper crowds along Ocean Avenue seem far away. Still, it is within easy walking distance of the town and even closer to Carmel's lovely white sand beach.

Although this is a small inn, the owners like to provide their guests with plenty of room. Thus, the accommodations are all two- and three-room suites, each with its own bath as well as antiques and items from the owners' private art collection. Each suite also has its own patio, and everyone enjoys the yard, which adds to the inn's charm. Since every suite has a refrigerator, and fresh coffee and orange juice are provided, you just need some rolls from one of Carmel's wonderful bakeries to make breakfast complete.

Highlands Inn

Distance: 124 miles from San Francisco, on Highway 1, 3 miles south of Carmel
Features: A big, sprawling, full-service inn; located on a high cliff with magnificent ocean views
Rates: For two people, $108 to $122 for fireplace cottage and $140 to $150 for lanai room with ocean view; rates are based on the American plan and include any two meals
Address: P.O. Box 1700, Carmel, California 93921
Phones: (408) 624-3801, or toll free (800) 682-4811 (California) and (800) 421-0000 (national)

First opened in 1916, the Highlands Inn is a fixture on the California coast that has grown until, to some, it may seem too big for a "wayside inn." Nevertheless, its many old admirers continue to think of it as a small and cozy inn, and in spite of the fact it has 105 rooms and the amenities of most full-scale hotels, its friendliness, Old World charm, and romatic location qualify it as an ideal stopover for travelers in the area.

It is a wonder how the inn's architects packed so much onto this precipitous hillside: a gift shop, a swimming pool, a chapel and outdoor wedding gazebo, and dozens of gardens containing a thousand varieties of flowers and plants. The large glass-walled restaurant and bar seem to hang right over the Pacific, and the hillside is packed with buildings containing a variety of pleasant guest accommodations. The only problem is parking, which can be difficult and is best left to the attendants at the entrance.

The Valley Lodge

Distance: 125 miles from San Francisco on the west side of Carmel Valley Village
Features: Carefully maintained, nicely appointed inn; quiet gardenlike setting; has its own swimming pool
Rates: From $38 for two people to $114 for four
Address: P.O. Box 93, Carmel Valley, California 93924
Phone: (408) 659-2261

The Valley Lodge has the advantage of being within walking distance of Carmel Valley Village, which has much of the same charm as Carmel itself, with many interesting shops and good restaurants, but only a fraction of the crowding and bustle. Besides that, it enjoys the valley's famous sunshine and good weather.

Of its thirty-one units, the garden patio rooms are least expensive, but each has its own deck or patio, open beam ceiling, and comfortable furnishings; some even have small kitchens. Next in size are fireplace suites, each with a wet bar, deck, and a hide-a-bed in the living section. These can be rented as a studio, or with one or two connecting bedrooms, making them suitable for two or three couples to share. Largest are fireplace cottages with living rooms, separate bedrooms, and kitchens, with their own hibachis on the deck.

Firewood is provided, and all rooms have color television, original watercolor paintings, and percolators. A community sauna and hot tubs are available as well as a lovely heated swimming pool. Beautifully planted grounds are a definite addition for the pleasure of guests.

The Gold Country

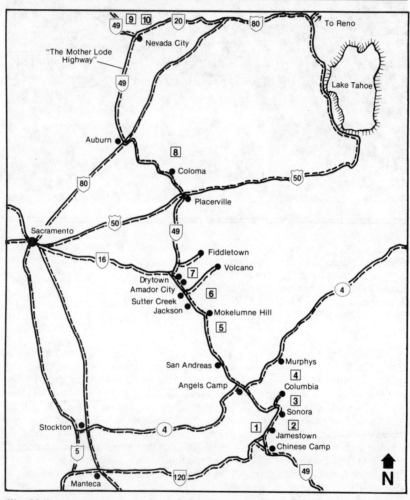

Wayside Inns

1	Jamestown Hotel		6	Sutter Creek Inn
2	The Gunn House		7	The Mine House Inn
3	City Hotel		8	Vineyard House
4	Murphys Hotel		9	National Hotel
5	Hotel Leger		10	Red Castle Inn

The Gold Country

Distance:

From San Francisco—125 miles to Jamestown; allow 2½ hours

Features:

A beautiful and historic part of California; one hundred fifty miles from end to end; ideal for a leisurely two- or three-day tour, with overnight stops at one or another of the many wayside inns

Activities:

Sight-seeing, photography, walking, and culinary adventures

Seasons:

Year around, but most pleasant during sunny weather

Rates:

The ten wayside inns included here have rates ranging from $24 to $53, with a median of $35 to $40, for two people

Addresses and Phones:

Refer to individual wayside inns at the end of the chapter

If you have two or three days to spare, want to slow down a bit, and harbor even a latent curiosity about the California gold rush, nothing could be more rewarding than a leisurely trip along the 150-mile length of the Mother Lode Highway (number forty-nine on the map). This road connects a string of quiet little towns separated from each other by a series of green rolling hills dotted here and there with pine and giant oak trees. Today, cattle and an occasional herd of sheep grazing in the sunshine are the most familiar sights along the way, making it hard to believe that over 130 years ago this gentle countryside was the site of one of the wildest, bawdiest, most colorful happenings in our history.

While meandering through these little towns, talking to the people who live here and checking out historical sites, the story will unfold of how the population in the Sierra Nevada foothills exploded in only a year's time from a mere handful of lumberjacks logging in the area to over 100,000 men. California was just a territory in 1848 when gold was discovered along the banks of the American River and the only big town, San Francisco, had a total population of 450. But once the word spread that gold nuggets could be picked off the ground, young men from all over the world dropped what they were doing and came pouring into California to seek their fortunes. As many of them showed signs of success, a new breed of scalawags followed: notorious robbers, high stake gamblers, and shady ladies, all hell-bent on separating the miners from their gold, either directly or indirectly. And therein lies many a tale — of fortunes made and lost, robberies, murders, hangings, and all forms of deceitful and heroic behavior on this raw frontier.

Incredible as it may seem, this notorious society met its end as quickly and dramatically as it had mushroomed into being. Within ten years after the forty-niners invaded the gold country they were almost all gone and the little towns that had sprung up on the original campsites were virtually deserted.

Today, these towns still are small, but each one is fiercely proud of its heritage and boasts of its own particular claim to fame—the biggest nugget, the oldest mine, the most hangings, or whatever. Also, there is a pervasive feeling that the inhabitants have made every effort to resist change and preserve not only the actual structures, but also the flavor of the past. The area thrives on stories and legends about the bad old days, many of which you will encounter again and again from the natives as well as from highway markers, plaques on historic old buildings, and voluminous gold rush literature.

If you should decide to explore this territory, don't bother to take along a television schedule because it is unlikely you will have a chance to use it. You will go a long way without even seeing a motel, and will stay instead in frontier hotels or charming inns, many of which are designated historic landmarks. The practice of turning old Victorian mansions into bed and breakfast hostelries was started in this area over fifteen years ago by Jane Way, the innovative owner of the Sutter Creek Inn. Now, there are a variety of such stopping points along the gold trail, each with its own particular fascination.

The way to see the gold country is to allot two or three days for the trip, beginning at one end and traveling leisurely through to the other, putting up each night at one of the inns. The little village of Jamestown, which bills itself as the "gateway to the Mother Lode," is in fact a good starting point for the tour, with Nevada City an ideal destination at the other end.

Jamestown is a tiny hamlet, but has many points of interest. Its history dates back to 1848 when the discovery of a seventy-five-pound nugget brought in a swarm of miners, the first of whom found they could actually pick gold from rocks with their penknives. The population soon swelled to six thousand, but as the gold disappeared so did the population. Today, even though the census taker can count only twelve hundred, the town has a sense of vitality due to an influx of artisans and craftsmen who have opened shops along the main street, offering fascinating browsing for tourists. Like so many of the early camps, Jamestown was ravaged by fire, but some of the old two-story buildings were restored and are still in use today. One of the most notable of these is the Jamestown Hotel.

Before moving on to Sonora, visit the homesite of the Sierra Railroad on the outskirts of Jamestown, where you will find a delightful display of original steam-powered engines and trains from the early days.

Upon reaching Sonora, a few miles north, you will find it has an entirely different feeling than Jamestown because Sonora's earliest settlers were from Mexico and their influence on the architecture and culture is still very much in evidence. The Gunn House, a charming inn with a rich historic background, is a perfect example of the adobe structures dating back to those days.

The Mexicans found an abundance of gold in Sonora and were leading a gay life until some disgruntled Yankees up north got wind of their good fortune and invaded their domain. Tensions ran high, leading to many confrontations that eventually ran the Mexicans out of town, but the spectacular gold finds continued and there was a constant influx of people. There were so many adventurers on the road between Stockton and Sonora, so the story goes, that a traveler could find his way at night by the light of their campfires.

Finally, Sonora became the hub of a cluster of lesser mining camps and gradually took on a few airs of refinement. Several nice hotels were built in town, featuring such unaccustomed luxuries as ice cream and drinks iced from snow packed in by mules from the mountains. But even as the miners got rich, they were often bored and found that leisure time was heavy on their hands. This gave rise to a dubious activity for which

One of Jamestown's fascinating stores

Sonora became famous. Every Sunday afternoon a bloody fight between a grizzly bear and a bull was staged to amuse the miners, who came from miles around to watch the barbaric affair.

The next little town, on a side road just a mile off the trail, is Columbia. Make a point to allow plenty of time for a visit here because Columbia is unchallenged as the finest surviving record of gold rush days. The town developed later than some of the other camps because, even though it had incredibly rich deposits of gold, it was not on a creek and water is essential for the placer, or hydraulic mining techniques favored in the early days before hard-rock mining developed. It was disgruntled Mexicans, kicked out of Sonora, who discovered the rich deposits. But again, the whites moved in right behind them when they heard the news. With a certain amount of ingenuity, a series of ditches, sloughs, and reservoirs was built, enabling the miners to bring in water, which in turn resulted in nearly a hundred million dollars in surface gold being taken out.

The town burned to the ground twice, but had been rebuilt in its present form by 1857. In 1945 the whole area became a state historical park and a beautiful job has been done of preserving the old mining town. Entire blocks of the original buildings have been closed off so you can wander down streets shaded by giant elms and trees of heaven (planted by the Chinese), past the blacksmith shop, still in operation, the Wells Fargo station, the apothecary, and the Chinese dry goods store, to mention just a few. The historic old City Hotel is right in the middle of the village and has as flourishing a business as ever putting up overnight guests and serving superb French cuisine. Nearby, the Fallon House Theatre, built in 1857, is now the scene of eight weeks of summer repertory productions of modern drama. Over a century ago, miners came to the same theater to watch Shakespearean drama performed by Edwin Booth and other great stars of the time.

Heading out of Columbia for Angels Camp, you will pass through a couple of little communities that are so small they are not even designated on some maps, but they played a large part in gold rush history. One of these is Tuttletown, where a historical marker tells of Mark Twain's sojourn in these parts when he was a young man. Just beyond town is a sign indicating where to turn off the highway for a visit to his rustic cabin on Jackass Hill where he wrote "The Celebrated Jumping Frog of Calaveras County" and gathered the material for *Roughing It*. It is not known for sure whether the acerbic young author gave the hill its name, but we do know there is some factual basis for it. It seems that the hill was a favorite spot for packers carrying supplies to camp overnight and inasmuch as there were often as many as two hundred jackasses on the hill at a time, it was the animals' nightly concert, or "donkey serenade," that gave rise to the colorful name.

Carson Hill is little more than a wide spot in the road, but it was the

Mark Twain's cabin on Jackass Hill near Tuttletown

point where the richest single discovery in the whole history of the gold rush was made. As a historical marker notes, it was here that a gold nugget weighing 195 pounds was found. Since gold was then valued at $16 an ounce, the nugget was worth $34,000. It is mind-boggling to think what it would be worth today.

Angels Camp is right in the heart of the Mother Lode and actually the place where the term (a Spanish expression meaning the main vein of ore) was originated. This roaring mining camp did not derive its name from impeccable virtue, but rather from its founder, George Angel, a bedraggled ex-soldier from the Mexican War who wandered into the area. Gold was so plentiful it could be picked off the ground and within a year there were four thousand miners with their tents pitched all along the banks of Angels Creek.

One of the town's legends concerns a local storekeeper who had a malfunctioning rifle. In order to clear it, he shot it into the ground, breaking open a rock revealing gold that led to a $10,000 discovery. Such stories were commonplace in those days and Mark Twain spent a lot of time in the 1860s roaming around the mining camps, Angels Camp in particular, to gather material for his tales. It was a bartender in the Angels Hotel that told him a yarn about a local man, Jim Smiley, who had a trained jumping frog. That tale led to one of Twain's first short stories. Angels Camp still has its annual Jumping Frog Jubilee, a lively week celebrating the event. Just outside of town a statue of Mark Twain stands in a lovely little park, which makes a delightful spot to picnic and relax for a bit.

Brete Harte was another writer who found rich material wandering around the mining camps. It was in this Calaveras country, mostly around Angels Camp, that the settings for his immortal stories, including "The Luck of Roaring Camp" and "The Outcasts of Poker Flat," can be identified. Such stories as "Mrs. Skagg's Husband" and "The Bell Ringer of Angels" were laid in the town of Angels itself.

From Angels Camp take a short side trip on Route 4 to Murphys, another town rich in the culture of the past. You can meander down the town's few streets, shaded by giant locust trees, and see many of the original old buildings, including the jail, an apothecary shop, the Wells Fargo building, and a quaint little white church that is beautifully preserved.

Long ago, the story goes, the Murphy brothers wandered into the area from Angels Camp and developed a knack for getting the local Indians to do their mining for them. To cinch the deal, one of them married the chief's daughter, and by the end of the year, both the brothers were millionaires.

Just as the gold supply was declining at Murphys, someone discovered a grove of giant sequoia trees nearby and this became enough of an attraction to warrant building a luxury hotel to handle the tourists. Murphys Hotel is still going strong and makes an excellent choice for a meal or overnight stop. The hotel also can provide details on another attraction of the area, the Mercer Caverns. It is a rare opportunity to see these labyrinthine passages, some still unexplored, filled with strange natural crystalline formations of stalactites, stalagmites, helictites, and columns.

After getting back on Highway 49, it is just a few miles to San Andreas, which is perhaps the most modern of the gold trail towns. There is very little left now from the old days, but San Andreas always will be remembered for bringing the notorious bandit Black Bart to justice, throwing him in jail for six years. Black Bart successfully robbed twenty-six Wells Fargo stages before the law finally caught up with him and, although Wells Fargo certainly did not agree, he was sort of a folk hero to many because he never fired a shot during his colorful escapades as a bandit. It came as a real surprise to everyone when it was revealed that in his everyday role, he was a mild-mannered clerk named Charles Bolton, the Clark Kent of the 1800s.

San Andreas was another one of those mining camps where Mexicans were the first settlers and then were rudely pushed out. One long suffering Mexican named Murietta, however, took deep offense—after a gang of Americans hung his brother, ravished his sweetheart, and horsewhipped him just for good measure—and became a Robin Hood type of bandit.

Seeking revenge on all who had mistreated him, he gave his booty to the poor. When bad luck finally caught up with him, he and his partner, Three-finger Jack, were ruthlessly murdered. Some enterprising soul cut off the head of one and the unusual hand of the other and, after pickling them in a jar of brandy, exhibited them around the state.

The next town, Mokelumne Hill, had the dubious distinction of being the wildest of the California mining towns. After a rich strike brought all kinds of miners, and the inevitable scalawags who followed them, into "Moke Hill," as it was commonly called, things got so uproarious that during one four-month period there was at least one murder a week, with five killings in one of those weeks. (Some of the mining claims near Moke Hill were of such small, postage-stamp size that the close proximity of competing neighbors often raised tempers and incited conflict.)

For awhile Moke Hill also had the distinction of being the county seat of Calaveras County, but when San Andreas managed to take the seat away, it turned out advantageously for Moke Hill. A saloon keeper there had the good sense to turn the empty county courthouse into an elegant hotel, which became the hub of the town's activity and the meeting place of many famous people. Today, the Hotel Leger is not only a lively and interesting place filled with lovely relics of the past, but also is the cultural and social center of town.

The next town is Jackson, which you will discover is very different from the other mining towns that you have been passing through. This is

One of the tall Kennedy wheels in Jackson

mainly because it was just coming into its own when the placer or surface mining camps were fast becoming ghost towns. Jackson prospered because the famous Kennedy Mine developed a deep, hard rock mining process that revolutionized the industry. Its main shaft was driven nearly a mile into the ground with a network of over a hundred miles of lateral tunnels.

Probably the most famous mining relic in the Mother Lode country is the Kennedy Tailing Wheel. Standing sixty-eight feet tall, it is one of four built in 1912 and is now on display at a park out on Jackson Gate Road. When the mine was in full operation, 75,000 gallons of water had to be pumped out of the mine shaft every twenty-four hours. The giant redwood spoke wheels were designed to lift 850 tons per day of the resulting sludge up the hill to an impounding dam to prevent pollution of the streams.

Jackson is also the home of the Amador County Museum, which is filled with mining relics and is easy to find because a bright red Baldwin steam engine stands prominently in the museum's front yard.

An interesting thing about Jackson is that the most prominent historical marker, still new and shiny, commemorates a rather unusual event. It seems that, even though Jackson got a late start as a town, the bawdy spirit lingered longer here than elsewhere—it was not until 1956 that the last bordellos were closed down. The bronze marker takes note of this historic occasion with a lament for what callous politicians can do to the most perfect example of free enterprise.

Another little town worth the time it takes to deviate from the main

Old Baldwin steam locomotive in Jackson

road is Volcano, a few miles from Jackson just off Route 88. Taking into consideration only the unrestored ghost towns, Volcano probably has more original old buildings standing than any of the others. Some are pretty decrepit, but others, such as the venerable St. George Hotel, are still in operation. The main attraction in the area, however, is Daffodil Hill, a local landmark close to Volcano that attracts many tourists each year in the spring when acres of golden hued flowers, growing from bulbs said to have been planted by Dutch settlers, burst into bloom.

Moving back up Highway 49, the next town on the map is Sutter Creek, a favorite of many, and a town with an aura all its own. Because of its central location, it got its start as a commercial center for neighboring settlements, but later, like Jackson, got into hard rock mining. These were the towns that lasted and, since Sutter Creek was built later and the town was prosperous, the structures were much more elegant than those in other gold rush towns. Many of the downtown buildings have ornate facades with balconies over the sidewalks, which greatly appeal to today's tourists attracted to shopping in the pleasant little row of stores and antique shops on the main street. Another interesting sight, located just a block from the center of town, is Knight's Foundry, the West's oldest foundry still run by water power. Castings are made every Friday (so they can cool over the weekend) and visitors are welcome to watch.

Looking at houses is also a favorite preoccupation with visitors as Sutter Creek has many lovely Victorian homes that have been beautifully kept up by their owners. One of the finest of these is the old-fashioned New England–style house at the north end of Main Street, turned into the well-known Sutter Creek Inn a number of years ago and now an excellent spot to stop overnight to relax and enjoy real hospitality.

Just a mile to the north in tiny Amador City, another famous old inn called the Mine House Inn is the most prepossessing building in town and also offers a fine respite for travelers. Although not known for commerce, the town does boast one industry, a small winery just off the highway, which invites passersby to come in and sample the product. Among other things, the Amador Winery produces miniature souvenir wine bottles commemorating the Mother Lode. One of its products is Madam Pink Chablis, named in honor of the gold country's former bawdy houses.

The next dot on the map is even smaller. Drytown today has a total population of seventy-nine, but is proud that, contrary to what its name might suggest, it had twenty-six saloons running full blast in its heyday. It seems that "dry" referred to the diggings. Drytown also is proud that it is the oldest town in Amador County.

From here on the road stretches out, with longer distances between the points of interest, which means all the more opportunities to enjoy the beautiful rolling green countryside.

Placerville is the next town of historical significance. Although most of the old mining towns have kept their original names, Placerville is an exception. It was first known as "Dry Diggin's" because the first summer that it was being mined the area suffered a drought, forcing the miners to carry dirt long distances to where water was available for panning. Soon, however, it got a new name. When some miscreants attracted by miner's gold were caught in the act of a robbery, they were hanged on the spot, the first recorded lynchings in the gold country. The town thereafter was known as Hangtown. This was only the beginning of a time when swift dispensation of justice and hangings were commonplace in the area.

Ironically, Hangtown did not come into full prosperity until the twilight days of gold mining. It was then that the same population turned eastward to follow the silver strike in Nevada and Hangtown become the main supply center for the trek to Virginia City.

Somewhere along the line, Hangtown took on the slightly more conventional name of Placerville and today it is a good sized, thriving town. As it, too, was a victim of a couple of devastating fires over the years, most of the old buildings are gone, but one point of interest remains. The Gold Bug Mine, just a mile from town in Bedford Park, as well as its nearby stamp mill, have been opened to the public for exploration. The mine is equipped with electric lights and it is exciting to wander its tunnels where you can actually see faint veins of gold in the rough quartz walls.

Placerville is a convenient point to pick up Highway 50 to Sacramento,

Gold Bug Mine entrance outside Placerville

leaving the Mother Lode country, or you can continue a few miles farther north to Coloma, the historic spot where gold was first discovered in the tailrace of John Sutter's sawmill and the rush began. A state-owned park alongside the highway commemorates the site with an authentic working reproduction of the old Sutter Mill, sitting on the bank of the American River exactly where the original one was built. A museum across the street contains other artifacts from those famous days.

One of the many stories told about what happened at Coloma during the height of gold fever concerned a solemn funeral ceremony for one of the miners. All progressed normally until someone spotted gold in the freshly dug grave. With that, the body was promptly put aside and everyone grabbed a shovel.

The gold supply was diminished early in Coloma and by 1851 it had settled back to the quiet little village it had been and is again today. Vineyard House, an old-time inn, is now the scene of most of the social activity in town. It has a lively saloon and serves dinner to more people each night than the total population of the town.

Nevada City, north about another forty miles, is an ideal spot to wind up your gold country tour, as it has a different kind of history than the mining towns to the south and is well worth visiting. Gold was discovered much later here and the original miners brought their women and children, accounting for more stability and less crime. When placer mining gave way to quartz mining, Nevada City prospered and became one of the three

Nevada City street scene

largest cities in California, along with San Francisco and Sacramento. (Los Angeles was just a sleepy little village at the time.) It was known as Nevada in those days, but when the territory of Nevada stole its title for the new state, the city fathers met and reluctantly added "City" to its name.

Today, Nevada City is a beautiful town built on a series of steep hills, with winding streets. Many of the handsome old buildings survive and there are some fine restaurants in town that cater to visitors. Two historic hostelries, both California landmarks, are at your disposal for an overnight visit. The National Hotel is right in the heart of town, and sitting high up on Prospect Hill is the romatic Red Castle Inn, painted bright red and bedecked with white gingerbread trim. From any one of the porches in this four-story Victorian you can look out over Deer Creek, where gold was first discovered in this part of the gold country, and see the town beyond with its picturesque buildings hugging the steep hillsides. It would seem there could be no finer vantage point from which to bid the gold country adieu.

Jamestown Hotel

Distance: 134 miles from San Francisco, in Jamestown.
Features: An authentic, hundred-year-old hotel, delightfully restored and decorated
Rates: $44 to $65 for two people
Address: P.O. Box 539, Jamestown, California 95327
Phone: (209) 984-3902

Standing on a prominent corner, this hotel has a buff-colored brick facade, and a typical balcony and ornate wooden railing reminiscent of many an old western movie. Recently restored, there is no longer a restaurant, but travelers are more than pleased with the heartier-than-usual breakfasts of fruit, juice, and homemade biscuits served in the sunny parlor.

The hotel's nine guest rooms have been redone with imaginative flair in a distinct departure from the heavy, plush feeling of many other old inns. Shiny brass beds with gay quilts are used throughout, and five of the nine accommodations have adjoining sitting rooms featuring white rattan furniture, with brightly colored cushions coordinated with the rugs and wallpaper. All rooms have private baths with old-fashioned pull-chain toilets and claw-leg tubs, reenameled in outlandish colors to match the overall decor.

The only modern addition is a hot tub built into a deck behind the hotel. Mod as it is, it is not hard to imagine an old miner climbing into a similar wooden vat for his Saturday night bath.

The Gunn House

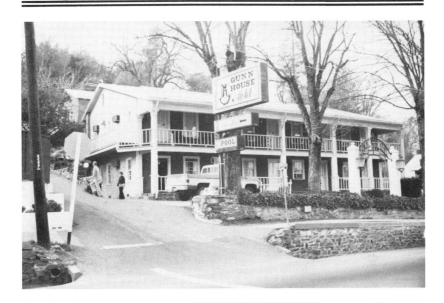

Distance: 136 miles from San Francisco, in Sonora
Features: Larger than most, this inn has twenty-seven rooms with private baths and a graceful pool in a flagstone terrace
Rates: $30 to $47 for two people
Address: 286 South Washington, Sonora, California 95370
Phone: (209) 532-3421

Today, the Gunn House is a lovely three-story inn created by expanding and restoring the first old two-story adobe built in Sonora. Dr. Gunn, one of the many young men lured by the Mother Lode, built it for his family, who then sailed around the Horn from the East. In those days, the Gunn House was a hotbed of political activity because the owner used one level to print an inflammatory newspaper that kept an already volatile populace continually stirred up.

The restoration did a beautiful job of preserving this historic landmark and turning it into a comfortable hostelry. A third level was added, while the terrace and pool were built into the hillside behind. The focal point today is an interior courtyard resplendent with Mexican wrought-iron grillwork from Sonora's early days, with a quiet little bar in the adjoining parlor.

All the rooms are furnished in walnut and mahogany antiques. The Gunn House has no restaurant, but coffee is served on the patio from eight to ten in the morning. Children are welcome and so are pets if the innkeeper likes the latter's looks.

City Hotel

Distance: 139 miles from San Francisco, in Columbia
Features: Elegantly restored and maintained by the state of California, this old
  hotel is a living historic monument
Rates: $44.50 to $53.50 for two people
Address: P.O. Box 1870, Columbia, California 95310
Phone: (209) 532-1479

Except for those who plan well ahead, a visit to City Hotel is usually limited to a meal in its elegant dining room, because overnight accommodations are booked months in advance. Even if you should have to settle for just a meal, however, it is worth the trip and you will feel the nostalgia of times gone by as you dine on the finest French cuisine at a table bedecked with flowers and a flickering oil lantern. Recently enticed from one of San Francisco's best-known restaurants, the chef is as special as the decor, and country living has only improved his culinary imagination.

A carpeted stairway with dark banisters leads from the dining room to the parlor and sleeping rooms above. Luncheon guests are invited to go up to see the beautiful antique furnishings between noon and three o'clock. During that time, the bedrooms are cordoned off, but the old, ornately hand-carved wooden beds and other exquisite items can be seen through the doorways. After three o'clock, those who were lucky enough to get reservations can take possession of their rooms. In the morning, they are served a continental breakfast in the parlor.

Murphys Hotel

Distance: 150 miles from San Francisco, in Murphys
Features: Beautifully preserved and steeped in history, with nine original rooms,
a restaurant and bar, plus twenty modern motel units
Rates: $35 to $63 for two people
Address: P.O. Box 329, Murphys, California 95247
Phone: (209) 728-3444

The little hamlet of Murphys likes to refer to itself as the "Queen of the Mother Lode," the focus of this pride in its glorious past being the venerable Murphys Hotel, which lays claim to being the oldest continuously operating hotel in California. Whether it is or not, its register dates back to a time when such illustrious folk as Mark Twain, Horatio Alger, and Ulysses S. Grant signed up for rooms. Another fascinating signature is that of C. E. Bolton, which in time proved to be the real name of the notorious bandit Black Bart. The claim is also made that the hotel is the one referred to in Bret Harte's story "Night in Wingdam."

Be all that as it may, the hotel is still a deservedly popular place to stay. The old rooms are furnished with antiques and the lobby, once known as The Ladies Parlor, where liqueurs were genteelly served, has the original wood stove and walls lined with cases of memorabilia from the past. The dining room serves three meals a day and the old Miner's Bar is still, just as in the past, the favorite gathering spot in town.

Hotel Leger

Distance: 120 miles from San Francisco, in Mokelumne Hill
Features: This historic hotel (pronounced "Leejay") includes a restaurant and
    bar, with a large swimming pool in the garden behind
Rates: $25 to $42 for two people
Address: Mokelumne Hill, California 95234
Phone: (209) 286-1401

With its canary yellow facade, flat roof, and ornate balcony supported by
white wooden columns, this hotel is another fine example of early western
architecture. Built over a hundred years ago, it now accomplishes the dual purpose
of helping preserve "Moke Hill's" romantic past, while serving as the hub of the
present community's activity.

Guests are put up in charming suites or rooms furnished with Victorian
antiques, and are invited to enjoy the cozy parlor and fine restaurant on the main
level. The garden swimming pool is also a source of much pleasure on sunny days,
which are frequent in this area. In the rear of the hotel, the Frontier Saloon is
probably as lively today as when it swarmed with miners, and still looks about the
same, with its massive, dark wood bar and its decorative stained glass, the small
marble-top tables, the rail-back chairs, and the inevitable old upright piano. Every
weekend live musical entertainment in the bar is popular, and in the Court House
Theater next door, a variety of entertainment is featured throughout the year.

Sutter Creek Inn

Distance: 125 miles from San Francisco, in Sutter Creek
Features: The original of all of California's wayside inns, this is still the pacesetter
for the rest
Rates: $35 to $48 weekdays; $45 to $68 weekends
Address: 75 Main Street, Sutter Creek, California 95685
Phone: (209) 267-5606

At the heart of the gold country, Sutter Creek was the most stable and genteel of the early mining towns. During the late 1850s some elegant establishments were built here, among the finest of which was the magnificent New England–style residence on Main Street, which is now the inn. Actually bigger than it looks from the street, it has seventeen rooms, all different because over the years the service buildings behind the main house have been imaginatively converted into rooms. Some are large, with fireplaces and private baths, others are smaller and share baths, but all are charming and, like the house itself, furnished in lovely antiques. An interesting innovation in a few rooms are beds suspended from the ceiling by chains that can rock gently at night.

The sunny drawing room is a perfect place for coffee, tea, or brandy before breakfast. Then at nine, a gong invites everyone to the flower-adorned harvest tables in the country kitchen, where an elegant breakfast, quite possibly the highlight of your stay, is served. (Rates include breakfast.)

The Mine House Inn

Distance: 123 miles from San Francisco, in Amador City
Features: A lovely Victorian brick building, on the west side of Highway 49, on a
hill overlooking town
Rates: $40 to $48 for two people
Address: P.O. Box 245, Amador City, California 95601
Phone: (209) 267-5900

Amador City is a pretentious name for what is virtually a ghost town. The inn,
however, was built as the offices of the booming Keystone Mining Company when
things were different, over a hundred years ago. Across the street you still can see
the rusty headrig at the entrance to a mine that turned out rich quartz ore until it
was closed in World War II.

Each of the inn's eight rooms is named after its original use. The Vault Room,
for example, still contains the old safe where bullion was kept until it was shipped
via Wells Fargo, and the Director's Room can be recognized by its high ceilings and
grand entrance onto the front balcony. All the rooms are spacious and airy, each
with an outside entrance and private bath. (The little chamber pots under the beds
are strictly for atmosphere, in keeping with the antique settings.)

A swimming pool on the side lawn is the only modern innovation, much
appreciated on hot days, as is the breakfast tray served each morning to guests in
their rooms.

Vineyard House

Distance: 134 miles from San Francisco, in Coloma
Features: An excellent restaurant trade and popular saloon are this inn's mainstays, as it has only seven rooms
Rates: $40 to $45 for two people
Address: P.O. Box 176, Coloma, California 95613
Phone: (916) 622-2217

Vineyard House is close to the site where all the excitement began in 1848 when Jim Marshall caught a glimpse of "color" in the tailrace of the sawmill he was building for Captain Sutter. Today, the town of Coloma seems so sleepy it is hard to believe Marshall's discovery triggered such a frenzied search for gold that men even dug up the town's main street in pursuit of the precious metal.

Vineyard House was built during those days as a hotel and private home. With vineyards nearby, the owner became a vintner of local note. His original labels are still on display in the front hall.

Today, the big Victorian house is the scene of more activity than the little hamlet seems capable of generating. Dinner often is served to as many as three hundred people, in five separate rooms, and on the porch in summer. The excellent food and the lively saloon draw people from all the neighboring towns.

The seven guest rooms all share baths and are named after celebrated personalities from the gold rush days. Continental breakfasts are included in room rates.

National Hotel

Distance: 150 miles from San Francisco, in Nevada City
Features: Located on the town's main street, this is another historic, well-preserved
frontier hotel, which has forty-three rooms, a restaurant, and a bar
Rates: $22 to $49 for two people
Address: 211 Broad Street, Nevada City, California 95959
Phone: (916) 265-4551

A grand hotel built in 1854, the National claims to be the oldest continually operating hostelry in California. (This is a claim also made by the Murphys Hotel some miles to the south, but in the spirit of the frontier, claims of being the biggest, richest, or oldest were routine affairs.)

The old brick structure is typical of the gold rush period, with furnishings in plush Victorian style. Burgundy colors are used generously in the rich upholstery, rugs, and wallpaper. The elegant second floor lobby was once the ballroom and is now filled with ornate furniture, including an old square grand piano that sailed around the Horn.

The western saloon downstairs contains an elaborate bar, originally built for the Spreckles mansion on Nob Hill. Millions of dollars of dust once passed across its well-worn top. The dining room also reflects the gold rush days, with coal-oil lamps decorating the tables and a huge candelabra overhead. Its excellent continental cuisine, however, is up to the standards of today's most modern hotels.

Red Castle Inn

Distance: 150 miles from San Francisco, in Nevada City
Features: This stately, red brick Victorian "castle" stands out on a hillside overlooking the city
Rates: $38 to $55 for two people
Address: 109 Prospect Street, Nevada City, California 95959
Phone: (916) 265-5135

From downtown Nevada City, you can't miss the tall, four-story neo-Gothic inn standing on Prospect Hill. From that vantage point it appears to be everything its name implies. Despite its size, there are just seven guest rooms (because the lower level is occupied by the innkeepers), but these rooms are spacious and imaginatively decorated with fine old furniture. Several rooms open onto balconies, others have fireplaces, and all, except for two quaint garret rooms, have private baths. On the hillside below are formal terraced gardens and a small pond.

The parlor has high ceilings and is elaborately furnished and full of clutter, making it a pleasant place in which to enjoy the continental breakfast set out each morning on the hall table. Along the hall is a fascinating display of wooden masks from all over the world.

Nevada City has good restaurants, and menus are available at the inn to help make your choice. To find the Red Castle, take the Sacramento Street exit from Route 49 and immediately look for an Exxon Station. Take a right turn at the station onto Prospect Street. The inn is on the left, a long block from the station.

The Lake Tahoe Area

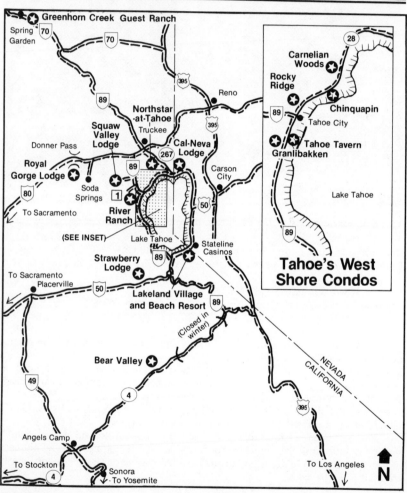

Greenhorn Creek Guest Ranch

Spring Garden

70

70

89

Reno

395

Northstar -at-Tahoe

Truckee

Squaw Valley Lodge

Donner Pass

Cal-Neva Lodge

267

Carson City

Royal Gorge Lodge

89

80

Soda Springs

1

To Sacramento

River Ranch

(SEE INSET)

Lake Tahoe

50

Strawberry Lodge

89

To Sacramento

Placerville

50

Stateline Casinos

Lakeland Village and Beach Resort

89

(Closed in winter)

Bear Valley

NEVADA

CALIFORNIA

49

4

395

Angels Camp

To Stockton

4

Sonora
To Yosemite

To Los Angeles

N

Tahoe's West Shore Condos

28

Carnelian Woods

Rocky Ridge

Chinquapin

89

Tahoe City

Granlibakken

Tahoe Tavern

Lake Tahoe

89

Wayside Inn

1 Mayfield House

Greenhorn Creek Guest Ranch

Distances:
> From San Francisco—248 miles; allow 5 hours
> From Reno—90 miles; allow 2 hours

Features:
> Family-oriented ranch in Plumas County's Feather River country; organized western fun from breakfast to bedtime

Activities:
> Horseback riding, pond and stream fishing, outdoor barbecues, hayrides, swimming, softball, square dancing

Seasons:
> April through November

Rates:
> Operates on American plan, with one price covering lodging, meals, riding; full-week visits encouraged by liberal discount program, with largest discounts in spring and fall—for example, discounted price per person in April and November $158 per week, in May and October $200, in July and August $340, with children approximately twenty percent less; add twelve percent service charge to all rates; no tipping; week runs from Saturday morning to Friday noon (6½ days)

Address:
> P.O. Box 11, Spring Garden, California 95971

Phone:
> (916) 283-0930

Lodge at Greenhorn Creek Guest Ranch

The constant whirlwind of activity at Greenhorn Creek Guest Ranch may seem somewhat incongruous with its peaceful setting in this part of the Sierras, but the activity is what the old-timers who come back year after year expect, and it goes on all summer long, with a new group of dudes checking in every week for the fun-packed program.

The ranch week begins Saturday and, as the guests drift in to register, they are immediately given a button with their first name on it to wear. From then on guests, wranglers, and all employees remain on a strict first name basis. The idea is to create a sense of belonging and conviviality, and it works wonderfully. Singles, couples, and family groups all fit quickly and easily into the scheme and are soon eating together, riding together, and playing together, and thoroughly enjoying newfound friendships.

After they get their buttons, new arrivals are given a tour of the ranch. Then they are shown to their quarters, where the first thing they will note is the mind-boggling calendar of events for the coming week posted on the wall. They may participate in whatever they want to, of course, but experience has been that almost everyone soon is involved with considerable gusto in all that goes on.

On the first night things start off with a bang with a "happy hour" get-acquainted party, followed by dinner and entertainment by the staff. The next day, after an initial riding lesson and the first trail ride, everyone hops aboard a wagon for a hayride and steak cookout in the woods, returning in time for a session of bingo, poker, and other card games held in the Greenhorn Saloon and Dance Hall.

By Monday, the dudes really get into the swing, and after the usual daytime riding activities, attend a candlelight dinner in the chuck house before retiring to the dance hall to dance until midnight.

The following evening, informality is once again the keynote with a bonfire sing-along after dinner. Then everyone roasts marshmallows while watching an impromptu talent show put together by the staff (and any of the guests who want to join in).

Wednesday is Rodeo Day, and all the guests participate in the events before turning out for a chicken barbecue in the late afternoon. Following that is a softball game in the corral with everyone joining in—men, women, children, and employees—and after that, for those who can still maneuver, square dancing begins at eight o'clock.

On Thursday night is a sort of grand finale when awards are ostentatiously given out for the "best rider," "most advancement," "happiest personality," and so on (everybody gets something), until finally the music starts for a real foot-stomping western country dance that lasts far into the night.

To some, the pace at Greenhorn might seem hectic, but it is really only as active as each person wants it to be. There is still plenty of time to fish in the pond and loaf by the pool. All the guests do their own thing, but in the final analysis, they all seem to have a very good time.

Routes and Distances

From San Francisco and Sacramento take Interstate 80 toward Reno. Soon, after crossing Donner Pass and descending along Donner Lake, you come to the intersection of Highway 89 at Truckee. Take 89 north toward Quincy. Fifty-eight miles from Truckee, just before reaching the little town of Spring Garden, look for a regular green highway sign indicating the Greenhorn Creek Ranch Road to the right. Follow the road two miles to the ranch.

People coming down from the north should take Highway 36 out of Red Bluff to where it joins Highway 89 east of Lake Almanor. Stay on 89 around the lake, through Greenville and Quincy to Spring Garden. The Greenhorn Creek Ranch Road will be encountered a short distance past Spring Garden. Total time from Red Bluff is approximately two and a half hours.

Accommodations

When you come in from the morning ride and tie your horse at his proper post (each fence post in the corral has a name on it; your horse will know his own place), it is just a short walk to the lodge and the row of cabins behind the chuck house.

The lodge is a two-story frame building with exterior verandas built to simulate an old-time frontier hotel. The lower level is devoted to the reception desk, offices, and a big parlor, with the guest rooms on the level above. Because of the single-price policy at Greenhorn, guests are assigned rooms in either the lodge or the cabins according to availability, although, if possible, the lodge rooms are given to adults, reserving the cabins for family groups with children. The lodge accommodations thus tend to be the quietest, which is appreciated by couples on a getaway. There are eight of these quarters, basically large hotel rooms, each with high open-beam ceilings, dark burnt-wood paneling, and a private bath. Not effusively furnished, they are nevertheless roomy and comfortable, with queen-sized beds and outside, on the veranda, a porch swing for lounging.

The sixteen cabins are furnished and finished in much the same manner, except that many have two adjoining rooms with two beds in each room for the benefit of larger groups.

The multitude of activities at Greenhorn makes it difficult to spend time in the room, except to sleep. Nevertheless, if two people both like to read in bed before dropping off they should bring along a small student desk lamp because if the rooms have a failing, it is the presence of only a single lamp on one side of the bed. This is a small inconvenience, however, and easily overlooked when one considers the overall bargain Greenhorn's American plan rates provide. Most places with riding, for instance, charge $6.50 per hour, or more, for time in the saddle. At Greenhorn, where you ride at least four hours a day, this would cost $26.00, but instead, during some seasons you pay less than that for room and board alone.

Greenhorn guests heading out on a trail ride

Fishing is second only to riding at Greenhorn

Activities

Anyone who truly wants to learn or improve on his horsemanship could not make a better choice for a week's vacation than the Greenhorn Creek Ranch. In the first place, all the riding is included in the basic cost of the vacation. There are no hourly extras. Secondly, the wranglers here take pride in becoming acquainted with the guests and helping them individually so they can sit a horse with confidence and ride all day in comfort. Finally, Greenhorn has a string of a hundred well-trained and responsive saddle animals (including some spunky ponies for the smaller kids), which ensures there will be a mount suitable for every level of ability.

Having grown up in cattle country and having worked horseflesh all his life, Joe, the head wrangler, looks, acts, and talks exactly as you would expect. He stresses safety first and wants no injuries to blemish his record. There are guest ranches, which, because of "insurance requirements," will not allow a pace faster than a walk. Joe snorts at this: "A ride can get strung out on the trail and the horses in back will break into a run to catch up. If the rider ain't learned to jog and lope, a fall can result. I teach everyone to handle a horse running, walking, and standing. That's safety." Besides, it is the only fun way. You are not a rider until you can run and enjoy it, and you do all that at Greenhorn.

The first day at the ranch is devoted to basic instruction for newcomers, and refreshers for experienced riders. Then everyone is divided into beginning, intermediate, and expert groups, and from then on there

The Wednesday Greenhorn softball game

are morning and afternoon rides each day for those who wish, or else day-long rides with lunch on the trail. Occasionally there are special events such as breakfast rides, evening cookouts, the rodeo, and maybe an old-fashioned impromptu horse race.

No doubt, the number two activity at the ranch is fishing. Nearly all the guests want to try their luck in the well-stocked trout pond that is formed by a dam near the corral. Of course, that is tame fishing (but at least no license is required in the pond). For the real thing, the Feather River, seven miles distant, is the place to go. The nearest point on the Feather will be found by driving left on the highway for six miles to the Sloat Road, where you turn right. Drive a short distance to a little cedar sawmill, go directly through its log yard, where you will come upon a bridge over the river. You can park there and proceed by foot to fish upstream or downstream on either bank.

Those with energy left after the daily rides and dances and ball games can hike the network of logging roads and riding trails crisscrossing the area. Or, in a more passive mood, they can retire to the saloon for a cold beverage, and, on hot days, to the adjacent pool for a dip or a bask in the sun.

Because of all these activities and the casual atmosphere, dress at Greenhorn is informal and western, meaning blue jeans, boots or heavy shoes with a heel for riding, a big hat for protection from the sun, and a sweater and Windbreaker to tie behind the saddle in the rare event the weather turns. The one exception is the Monday candlelight dinner, where ladies often like to wear long dresses or skirts and men fancy shirts because the affair is followed by a dance. And bring swimsuits, of course, for the pool.

Dining

Dining is always fun at the ranch where all the meals are served family style and no choices have to be made. A dude's only responsibility is to show up for dinner at the chuck house within fifteen minutes after the cook bangs out a summons on his big iron triangle. The schedule is more flexible at breakfast, which is served anytime between 6:30 and 10:00. Lunch is prepared for those not out on the trail about noon, or whenever the morning riders get back to the ranch.

The chuck house, which is furnished with tables made of half rounds of pine surrounded by big, heavy captain's chairs, has a warm and friendly atmosphere. When the meals are served buffet style, guests help themselves and sit wherever they choose, but at other times place cards are arranged to mix up the seating, allowing guests to get better acquainted.

The only times guests do not eat in the chuck house are when there is a barbecue out on the lawn or a meal from the chuck wagon out on the trail. On the night of the hayride, for example, there is a steak cookout in the woods and, of course, the all-day trail riders also get their lunches from the chuck wagon. It is always a treat when these riders catch the first whiff of hamburgers sizzling on the grill as they approach the forest dell, and find rustic tables already spread with the picnic fare.

Greenhorn's Wednesday barbecue

Royal Gorge
Nordic Ski Resort

Distances:
> From San Francisco—178 miles; allow 3½ hours
> From Reno—44 miles; allow 1 hour

Features:
> Rustic remote lodge; located at the crest of the Sierras and accessible only on skis or by sleigh; offers preeminent Nordic ski program with exceptional country French cuisine

Activities:
> Cross-country skiing, "hot tubbing," sauna, card games, reading

Seasons:
> Depends on the snow; usually mid-November through mid-May

Rates:
> Rates cover transportation into lodge, lodging, meals, ski lessons, and hot tub and sauna; weekend program (Friday through Sunday afternoon), $130 per person; midweek program (Wednesday afternoon through Friday afternoon), $115 per person; special programs for major holidays and three-day weekends; midweek program has fewer people and subsequent advantages

Address:
> P.O. Box 178, Soda Springs, California 95728

Phone:
> (916) 426-3871

Sleigh takes guests to Royal Gorge Lodge

When you check in at the Soda Springs headquarters of the Royal Gorge Resort, you launch yourself on a genuine Nordic ski adventure. This type of cross-country skiing experience, modeled after European ski touring schools, is available in only three places in the United States, and the other two are in the eastern section of the country.

It all begins when you and the other skiers congregate at the Royal Gorge Ski Shop. After checking in, you are promptly fitted with the appropriate skis and boots, if you need them, or you can spend the time getting acquainted with the others with whom you will be spending the next couple of days. The staff is well organized and the program clicks off with rarely a hitch. When everyone is checked in and fitted for equipment, the skis and baggage (and probably Mountain, the lodge's big Newfoundland mascot) are loaded on a pickup and the guests follow in their own cars to the trailhead. Upon reaching the trailhead, a half mile away, everyone turns around and parks the cars bumper to bumper along the road headed out of the area. (The wisdom of this maneuver will manifest itself later.)

A bright red sleigh, pulled by a snow cat, waits at the trailhead to deliver the new batch of skiers to the lodge. After all the duffel bags, sleeping bags, and skis are loaded in the snow cat, everyone climbs aboard the sleigh and wraps up in big Argentine fur lap robes to get cozy for the two-mile trip through the woods.

In the peak of the season the side walls of the rustic lodge, built in 1921 as a hunting lodge, are banked with snow right up to the roof, and when you approach, only a dark triangle containing the entrance door is discernible. Inside, a roaring fire and warm hospitality await. If this is a midweek visit, you will be served hot tea or coffee and hors d'oeuvres to hold you over until dinnertime. Weekenders arrive at a later hour and will find hot spiced wine and a delicious cheese fondue in lieu of dinner.

Thus the adventure begins. The next two days will be a delightful and strenuous experience. At the end of the trip there will be no sleigh ride back to civilization because everyone skis out, ending the trip with feelings of exhilaration and accomplishment. The staff comes out with the luggage, loaded on the snow cat, and is on hand to help get the cars out if it has snowed heavily. It is then that the logic for the parking arrangement becomes clear: dig out the first car in line and the rest can drive away.

Routes and Distances

The main interstate highway, I-80, from San Francisco to Reno, runs directly past Soda Springs, close to Donner Summit. At Soda Springs, take the well-marked exit and go east on old Highway 40 for approximately one mile, past the Donner Summit Lodge and the Donner Trail Store, to a large old hotel building. There, you will see the Royal Gorge Nordic Ski Resort sign prominently marking the check-in point.

Accommodations

Nobody on first arrival is quite prepared for the Royal Gorge Lodge. You enter through a tunnellike entrance into the ski waxing shop, then go up a narrow staircase to the bunk room, and back down another staircase to the big living room–dining room.

The entire lodge is heated solely by wood. A deep stone fireplace at one end takes logs so big a man can barely lift them. In the center of the room is a sheet-iron stove set on a brick hearth, and at the far end is a second stove. All of these are kept stoked and hotly burning, serving two purposes: to heat the building and to dry out wet ski gear between sessions. The end of the room, toward the fireplace, is filled with comfortable sofas, lounge chairs, and big pillows for casual lounging. The other end contains seven eight-place informal dining tables.

Above the main room is the bunk room, divided into four sections by gaudy silk banners suspended from the ceiling. Each section contains six to eight iron bunks, mostly double-deckers. After arriving on the sleigh, you unload your gear and climb the stairs to the bunk room where you claim a bunk by piling your equipment on it. You may find yourself bunking with utter strangers, male or female, and in close proximity, too. Besides that, the bathroom facilities at the bunk room entrance are co-ed and there are no showers, so the hot tub, at the end of a brisk hundred-yard dash across

Skiers assemble in front of Royal Gorge

the snow, is the bathing alternative.

These are just some of the things that make Royal Gorge different. You eat with the others, ski with them, bunk with them, and use the hot tub with them, but remember: this lodge is deep in the Sierras, and it is surprising how many first-rate amenities it *does* manage to provide. At any rate, if you bump elbows a bit because of the close quarters, you also, in two days, will get to know a number of people well, making some good friends, and you will have had an experience that you will remember long after ordinary vacations have been forgotten.

Because of these special circumstances, be sure to bring a sleeping bag, a towel for the hot tub, a robe to wear to the bathroom, and a flashlight to use for finding your way through the bunk room at night.

Activities

About eight on the evening you arrive, after hot mulled wine and dinner (if it is a midweek session), the call rings out for moonlight skiers. From then on it is ski, ski, ski until, on the afternoon of the final day—and even then—you ski out to the trailhead.

On the morning after arrival, first thing before breakfast, you have a choice. You can put on your skis for a half-hour appetite-building tour, or you can join the others on the living room floor and, led by one of the instructors, do vigorous stretching exercises. After breakfast at ten, all the

Hot tub in woods at Royal Gorge

skiers assemble in front of the lodge where they are broken into groups, roughly according to ability, for a morning of instruction. (Those who prefer it are free to strike out on their own, but most like to take the opportunity to brush up on their skills.) An instructor takes each group to a practice area, where basic cross-country striding technique, the kick, the glide, turns and stops, uphill and downhill get a thorough going over with plenty of opportunity for individual practice. At noon, all groups return to the lodge for a sumptuous lunch.

At two, it is out into the snow again to put the morning's lessons to practical use. The afternoon session typically will be about a two-hour tour over one of the loops in Royal Gorge's 125 miles of groomed trails. Skiers are afforded the opportunity to enjoy the high Sierra scenery on these trail tours. Many people think wintertime is the loveliest time of year in this unbelievably pretty country, and gliding silently through the snow is the way to make the most of it. The instructor leading the tour watches the group and stops occasionally to make suggestions and recommendations about technique and trail etiquette.

Returning to the lodge about 4:30, some go across to the sauna and hot tub while others stretch out with a cup of coffee to read or play games by the fire. The hot tub and sauna are in a separate small hut a hundred yards from the lodge. You traipse across the snow and change when you get there. There is only a single changing room and, as the tub and sauna are both co-ed, people have to work out the arrangements, which they always seem to do. (From 8:00 to 9:00 P.M. there is generally a special ladies' hour in the hot tub, for those who prefer segregation.)

After dinner is a time for lounging around the fireplace and stoves, conversing, playing games, or reading. Sometimes one of the more talented instructors gets out a guitar and an impromptu sing along may start. The more avid skiers, however, tear themselves away for the nightly moonlight tour, which is an experience to be enjoyed at least once. The woods are different at night, even quieter and more beautiful in the soft light. Even if there is no moon, the stars generally provide enough light once the eyes become adjusted. The flat light makes it difficult to see bumps or hollows in the snow and you learn to ski instinctively, feeling for imperfections in the surface and adjusting to them with the knees.

On the second morning the exercise session and prebreakfast tour are repeated. After breakfast one of the instructors conducts an interesting seminar in front of the fireplace to explain and demonstrate how to choose cross-country equipment. Then, it's on to the next to the last ski session, usually a longer tour on the trail to Kidd Lake or one of the other more scenic routes where the vistas look out over the valley to mountains beyond. The skiers work hard and are ready for a big lunch at noon, when they get back to the lodge. After that, they pack up, load their gear into the snow cat, and ski out on their own over the forty-five-minute run on Yuba Trail back to the trailhead and the cars.

Dining

It almost would seem more appropriate to discuss dining under "Activities" because eating is second only to skiing as a major happening at the lodge. According to the trim ski instructors, the reward for a rigorous day of skiing is the ability to indulge, without adding extra pounds, in the seemingly endless layout of elegant food encountered at every meal.

There is only so much that can be said about food, but the country French cooking at Royal Gorge deserves extravagant praise, especially considering that all the chef's supplies have to come in by snow cat.

Skiers arise early at the lodge and after morning warm-up exercises line up at a sumptuous breakfast buffet: mixed fresh fruit, melon slices, yogurt decorated with sliced apples, steaming hot cereal, hard-cooked eggs, Swedish pancakes, French bread with cheese, freshly baked flaky croissants with blueberries and jellies, and orange juice, coffee, and tea.

After a morning of skiing, you will find it possible to eat again, even though it seemed impossible a few hours earlier. Wine and lemonade are enjoyed before sitting down to lunch with other guests and with one of the ski instructors at the head of each table. He serves hot soup from a tureen and warm French bread and butter are passed. This seems just right for a skiers' lunch, but it is only the beginning. Another buffet spread offers several elegant salad selections, caviar, liver pâté, cheese, and crackers ad infinitum. It is no wonder that after lunch there is at least one sleeping body collapsed on each of the big overstuffed couches around the fireplace and stoves, resting up for the activity to follow.

After more hours on the cross-country trails in the afternoon, nothing is more rewarding than returning to the lodge, finally taking off your boots, and gathering with other guests around a big caldron of hot spiced wine while awaiting the chef's next extravaganza.

When dinner is announced, the instructors become waiters and deftly serve all the guests before each takes his place at the head of one of the tables. It is all very colorful, with bright red checkered cloths on the table and kerosene lamps lighting the area, with a little help from the fire glowing in the big stone fireplace. Dinner is another gourmet affair, ending with delicate French pastries made in the lodge's own kitchen. It is at about this time that you decide the name of the place refers not to the geographical location, but rather to the dining experience—a royal gorge.

Squaw Valley Lodge

Distances:

    From San Francisco—200 miles; allow 4 hours

    From Sacramento—115 miles; allow 2½ hours

Features:

    Centrally located in the huge Squaw Valley recreational complex; the lodge originally was built for the 1960 Winter Olympics; now a full, year-round resort

Activities:

    Downhill and cross-country skiing in winter; tennis, swimming, hiking, mountaineering, fishing, horseback riding, arts and crafts festivals in summer; golf, gambling, river rafting nearby

Seasons:

    Year around

Rates:

    $21 to $80 for two people in winter; $14 to $32 May through October

Address:

    P.O. Box 2393, Olympic Valley, California 95730

Phone:

    (916) 583-0121

Olympic Village in Squaw Valley

Squaw Valley's worldwide renown stems from hosting the Winter Olympic Games in 1960. The reasons the valley was chosen for the Olympics are obvious: the powder snow of a high location and the magnificent adaptability of the terrain to all major winter sports, everything from ski jumping and downhill to the biathlon and bobsledding. A big coliseum was built to house the ice skating and hockey facilities, and a whole village was constructed to feed, house, and cater to the multitudinous needs of thousands of athletes and spectators.

The Olympics are long since over, but all of the natural conditions and buildings, so eminently suitable for the Games, now admirably lend themselves to recreational winter activities. These, plus the relative closeness of the area to big population centers, have made "Squaw" California's best-known and one of its most heavily utilized ski areas.

For a long time, though, when it came to summer sports, Lake Tahoe just a few miles to the east always commanded the attention of the vacationing public. Years passed before people began to discover that the flat valley ringed with mountains, only fifteen minutes away, had so much to offer. Now, all that is changing. A good pool, tennis courts, and riding stables, and just plain beautiful country, are attracting year-round attention to Squaw Valley.

For overnight visitors, there are several places to stay, but for making the most of the area, in winter or summer, the Squaw Valley Lodge undoubtedly offers the best accommodations and is most centrally located. The main cable-car lift, which goes up to High Camp, flanks the lodge on one side, while the big Olympic House complex, with all the restaurants and bars and shops, is on the other. The tennis courts and pool are immediately behind, and lodge guests have their own private parking area, especially desirable at the height of the ski season.

The first thing you see at Squaw Valley is a tall monument topped with the five interlocking Olympic rings and decorated with the emblems of all the 1960 participating nations. Tradition, you soon learn, is terribly important here. The flags and emblems are repeated again and again in the many eating and drinking places throughout the area. All this color and reminders of past glory, plus the size and magnificence of the valley and surrounding mountains, leave impressions that are not easily forgotten.

Routes and Distances

From San Francisco and Sacramento take Interstate 80 east toward Reno, but turn off at Truckee and go south on Route 89. Proceed ten miles and look for the well-marked right turn to Squaw Valley. The lodge is in the center of the complex, one and a half miles from the turnoff.

Accommodations

Change is in the wind at Squaw Valley. In the winter the slopes have

Spring skiers at Squaw Valley enjoy sunshine

always been inundated with crowds of day skiers, but it is clear that more people want to stay for longer than just the day. A move is under way, with new construction already evident, to convert Squaw Valley gradually into a full-destination winter and summer resort on the order of Aspen or Sun Valley. Ultimately, there will be brand new accommodation units and rental condominiums, and the present lodge undoubtedly will be replaced or completely redone. But this will take time, and for the next few years the present configuration of lodge accommodations probably will remain with but minor changes.

Thus, at well over thirty years of age, some of the present lodge rooms may show some wear. Nevertheless, the lodge has the benefits of an ideal location and a wide range of rates to fit every purse. The least expensive rooms, for instance, are tiny "share-bath" units, popular with young skiers who just want a place to sleep. After that in price are bungalow rooms, which are not fancy but have private baths. Then there are hotel rooms, which are much larger and more comfortable and include color televisions. Finally, the most expensive, and correspondingly the nicest, accommodations are a number of two-room suites. The hotel rooms, with two queen-sized beds, can sleep up to four people, but the suites can take as many as six—sardine fashion, of course.

Activities

In addition to being an area of awesome natural beauty, Squaw Valley is grandiose in scale. Over five thousand acres of ski trails crisscross the slopes of five major Sierra peaks rising steeply from the valley floor. Within its confines are two distinct ski areas, each with a multitude of runs of all degrees of difficulty, served by twenty-five lifts, a gondola, and one of the world's largest aerial trams.

The lower Olympic House area starts on the valley floor at 6,200 feet, with multiple lifts serving many runs. The giant tram, the gondola, and the Super Squaw lift transport skiers 2,000 feet higher to a second area that cannot even be seen from the valley floor. At this 8,200-foot level other lifts, beginning at High Camp and Gold Coast, carry skiers right up to the peaks of the surrounding mountains.

Over fifty instructors are available at Squaw Valley to help individual skiers and groups with everything from mastering the basics to executing the advanced runs, some of which rival the most expert slopes in the world.

During the season, when there is enough snow on the valley floor, cross-country skiing is also popular in the Papoose Ski Area, where trails lead out over the lower levels of the valley.

An indoor ice arena, built by the government to accommodate the Olympiad ice contests in 1960, always has been available for public use until just recently, when it had to be closed down because necessary major renovations needed to be made. At the time of this writing, its future is

Squaw Valley lifts and a gondola ascend to major Sierra peaks

somewhat uncertain, but a new management group has taken over, and supposedly will reopen the arena soon.

In summer, lodge guests need only step outside their rooms to enjoy an Olympic-sized pool and six well-kept tennis courts. The courts belong to a local tennis club, which charges lodge guests a nominal fee to play, but welcomes them to participate in the clinics and attend the exhibitions and tournaments that take place throughout the summer.

Riding is a favorite pastime in the valley and an excellent string of horses is available at the Equestrian Center just a few blocks from the lodge. Guided trail rides into the mountains and overnight camping trips can be arranged with short notice.

Hiking and mountaineering also are popular with summer visitors. Many hikers take the tram up to the 8,200-foot level and strike out from there for overnight trips to one of the many beautiful alpine lakes in the area. Shirley Lake, which lies in the saddle between Emigrant Peak and Granite Chief, is especially lovely and a good destination for a first hike in the area.

Trout fishing in the mountain streams and along the Truckee River is an attraction for fly fishermen. A bonus is the opportunity to take part in seminars on fly casting, which are conducted by an expert on summer weekends.

Although there is no golf course in the valley, it is just eight miles to

Tahoe City where there is a game nine-hole municipal course. Tahoe City is also the place to rent rafts for floating down the Truckee River, a sport that is rapidly growing in popularity.

For those who enjoy less strenuous activity, numerous arts and crafts festivals are held in the valley throughout the summer. The lovely climate and beautiful environment also make just plain loafing and enjoying the scenery a pleasure.

In the evening Squaw Valley has its own theater, which shows a movie twice nightly, as well as a large number of bars offering live entertainment. And, of course, the casino at Cal-Neva is just twenty miles away, a mere nothing to those who like to try their luck at gambling.

Dining

Luckily for the hordes of skiers that invade the valley, many little delis and short order food shops were built to accommodate the crowds that came to watch the Games. In Olympic House alone there are at least five concessions serving pizzas, hamburgers, strudels, and sandwiches, and at the Gold Coast Lodge, at the top of the gondola lift, there is another deli and a taco hut.

More substantial lunches are served year around at two restaurants in High Camp, the station at the top of the aerial tram. (The only drawback is that you must purchase a six-dollar ticket for the ride up, but it nevertheless is a worthwhile experience at least once. The panoramic views of

Squaw Valley slopes offer good hiking in summer

mountain peaks in every direction and Lake Tahoe nestled among them to the east are something to see.) One of these restaurants, The Granite Chief, serves a large selection of excellent sandwiches and salads, but the big favorite is a fruit, cheese, and nut board served with white wine. The Summit House specializes in early California cooking, with such favorites as tamale pie, enchiladas, and stuffed green peppers, served cafeteria style.

Besides these breakfast and lunch places, there are three full-service dinner houses in the valley. The Olympic House, next to the lodge, has a nice dining room called The Valley Floor on the second level. It is open every night and offers a well-balanced menu, with prime rib that is especially good.

Mario's across the street from the lodge in the Village Inn, serves a good dinner and has an especially cozy bar where you can count on a roaring fire on cold evenings.

A new establishment, The Christy Inn, about a quarter mile from the lodge, is delighting guests with truly gourmet cooking. The owner-managers are a young couple who pay meticulous personal attention to both preparation and service of each meal. They are able to do this because their elegant little dining room contains no more than ten or twelve tables. Each night several exotic specialties are offered in addition to the regular menu. The chef has a way with sauces, especially with seafood dishes, and no matter whether you choose swordfish or scallops or scampi (to name only a few), you will not be disappointed. The Christy Inn also has a good selection of the usual meat dishes. The salads are a la carte, but an excellent homemade soup is served with the dinner.

River Ranch

Distances:

From San Francisco—200 miles; allow 4 hours

From Sacramento—115 miles; allow 2½ hours

Features:

Actually an inn rather than a ranch; nestled close to the Truckee River and centrally located in the Tahoe area; characterized by informality, friendliness, and a fine dining room

Activities:

Skiing in winter; river rafting, river swimming, fishing, hiking, golf, bicycling, horseback riding, kayaking in summer; gambling nearby

Seasons:

Year around

Rates:

$25 to $45 for rooms sleeping from two to five people

Address:

Box 197, Tahoe City, California 95730

Phone:

(916) 583-4264

River Ranch on the Truckee River

Ask any native in the Tahoe area for suggestions on where to spend your Sierra vacation and you will find River Ranch high on just about every list. The reason is that in winter or summer, it is in the heart of all the activity in the area. Contrary to what its name might imply, it has never had anything to do with any type of ranching. Rather, it is a charming old lodge built during the postdepression days in a sharp bend in the Truckee River. Something about this setting, where early pioneers in their Conestoga wagons liked to camp while traveling through the area, establishes an informal and cozy atmosphere.

In winter skiers like to gather in the bar, a big circular room canti-levered over the river, after the lifts shut down on the nearby slopes. Since River Ranch is right at the entrance to Alpine Meadows and just a few miles from Squaw Valley, every skier coming off the mountain passes by, making it a natural après-ski gathering spot. By five o'clock on any winter day, the lounge begins to fill with skiers listening to music at little tables overlooking the river or grouped around the cozy fireplace.

In summertime the focal point of activity switches to the broad, sunny, concrete patio that covers the entire area between the lodge and the river's edge. It is here that all the river rafters from Tahoe City terminate their four-mile voyage, because beyond this point the river is full of rapids and is hazardous to navigate. All day long, rafters drift into the deep pool in front of River Ranch and clamber up over the rock wall onto the patio to rest and enjoy a cool drink and a barbecue lunch. It makes a colorful scene, and is fun to be a part of, even if you are just an observer.

Routes and Distances

Take Interstate 80 east from the Bay Area, over Donner Pass to Truckee. At Truckee, exit to the right on Highway 89 toward Tahoe City. Three-quarters of the way to Tahoe, a mile past the Squaw Valley turnoff, the highway intersects the Alpine Meadows Road leading to the Alpine Meadows Ski Area. At the corner, immediately beyond the turn on the right side of the highway (and impossible to miss), is River Ranch.

Accommodations

The rambling wooden building with its unusual, intricately cut, wood-shingle siding is the first notable thing you see at River Ranch. This old-style exterior conveys something of the informality and friendliness for which River Ranch is known. The rambling layout was designed to fit the building into the crook of the river in such a way that that the dining room, all the sleeping rooms, and, most particularly, the bar, would have pleasant views of the water tumbling over rocks, while at night, guests would be lulled by its gentle murmur.

The newest rooms in the inn, numbers twenty-one through twenty-six, take full advantage of this by having large sliding-glass doors opening onto their own private balconies practically overhanging the stream. Particularly well suited for couples, these six rooms are probably the most desirable units, each having a queen-sized bed, attractive furniture, and an individual outside entrance. All of the fifteen other rooms were completely remodeled and redecorated in 1980, and most of these also have individual outside entrances, although a few open off a hall in the second story. Instead of private balconies, these rooms share verandas or porches facing the river. Some of them have more than two beds to accommodate whole families, if need be, in one room. No two of these rooms are alike, being of different sizes and shapes and individually decorated with a variety of patterned wallpapers and bedspreads and antique furnishings. A basket of fresh fruit found in every room is an unexpected added touch.

Being just around the corner from the two ski areas, River Ranch is always attractive as a place for skiers to stay. Those who are content with just a place to sleep at a good price will be glad to know that River Ranch has four special rooms, not included in those mentioned above, just for them. These are small, plainly furnished bunk rooms, with two double-deck beds that sleep four people. The cost per person is very low.

Activities

River Ranch has become famous for introducing guests to river rafting. A free bus takes rafters five miles up the Truckee, where they rent

Rafters arrive at River Ranch's patio

rafts and embark on a memorable two-hour trip. Drifting over mostly smooth water with just a few spots of white, they travel through typically majestic Sierra forests and finally end up at River Ranch's large pond below the broad patio area. This trip has become so popular that the bus, which also returns the rafts, must run back and forth all day, starting at nine and ending at six. There is even an enterprising photographer along the way who takes color shots of the rafters as they float by, and has finished eight-by-ten prints ready by the time the trip is over.

Along with the rafters, kayakers are a common sight on the river and swimming in the Truckee is another favorite local sport. The river is the only outlet of Lake Tahoe, and the water flowing out is always clear and fresh as it passes River Ranch. The best place to swim is in the same pond where the rafters wind up. The Truckee also can afford good trout fishing, except where rafting spooks the fish. Upstream near Tahoe City and downstream past River Ranch are the places to try.

In the high country around Alpine Meadows and Squaw Valley are endless hiking opportunities. One of the nicest trips for unsurpassed scenery is Shirley Canyon at Squaw. A pretty little lake on top makes a good destination for a picnic lunch. Or, for a bit of climbing practice close to home, go directly across the highway from River Ranch and climb straight up scree slopes and rimrock outcroppings to the ridge above. It is a tough scramble, but the wide-angle view of Alpine Meadows that you get from the top is worth it.

If horseback riding is your sport, there are miles of trails back into the Sierra Nevadas to explore. The nearest place to obtain horses is at Alpine Stables, a half mile up Alpine Meadows Road. For golf, Tahoe City's nine-hole course is five minutes away, and the two excellent Incline Village courses are not over a half hour's drive away.

Bring your bicycle if you can. A splendid asphalt bike trail closely follows the edge of the Truckee all the way from Tahoe City to within two hundred yards of River Ranch. Joggers, of course, can share this path and particularly enjoy the traffic-free chance to take in the scenery.

All winter long River Ranch is skiers' headquarters. A chapter in this book is devoted to Squaw Valley, just a few miles away. Even closer is Alpine Meadows, which is a smaller area but has a higher percentage of difficult runs, and therefore is a favorite of the experts.

Nobody can get away from the Tahoe area without crossing over to Nevada at least once to try his or her luck at gambling. That, too, is less than a half hour distant at Cal-Neva or the Hyatt-Tahoe on the north end of the lake. Good luck!

Dining

It is apparent on first seeing the dining facility at River Ranch that it is prepared to serve many more people than just the guests staying at the lodge. Four separate dining alcoves, two with fireplaces, run the length of

Alpine Meadows is five minutes from River Ranch

the building, and each has a window wall looking out over the patio to the river. Divided this way, the dining areas reflect an intimacy that is further enhanced by candlelight.

Notwithstanding this romantic atmosphere, the dining room is always bustling, because River Ranch is one of the most popular spots in the Tahoe area. The reasons are very simple: excellent food served in a nice setting for reasonable prices. The menu is straightforward, and features barbecued beef ribs, short ribs, and spareribs. In addition, there is an array of steak and seafood selections, and several veal and chicken dishes. All dinners are served with homemade soup, green salad, and hot bread.

In wintertime, dinner is the only meal served to the public. For guests of the lodge, however, an informal continental breakfast is laid out on the sideboard in the dining room, where people can help themselves anytime they like. No lunch is served since most of the guests are skiers and are up on the mountain.

In summer, it is a different scene altogether. Beginning at 11:00A.M., lunch and a variety of beverages are served on the patio to the hungry rafters disembarking at the lodge after their trip down the river (and to the others who turn out just to watch the fun). All day long the huge patio is filled with people sitting around picnic tables and in deck chairs enjoying fresh fruit daiquiris and other beverages from the outdoor bar, and barbecued chicken and hamburgers and hot dogs from the giant patio grill. This activity continues right up until six, when the rafting stops, the dining room opens, and the fun moves inside.

Northstar-at-Tahoe

Distances:

From San Francisco—197 miles; allow 4 hours

From Sacramento—112 miles; allow 2 hours

Features:

A complete resort, meticulously planned to take fullest advantage year around of its location high in the Sierra Nevadas

Activities:

Downhill and cross-country skiing, golf, tennis, swimming, par course, spa, sauna, exercise room, horseback riding, hiking; gambling and casino entertainment nearby

Seasons:

Year around; regular season—1 July through mid-September and December through April; value season—1 May through June and mid-September through November

Rates:

For two people, $70 to $100 for regular season and $35 to $55 for value season; two- to four-bedroom condos and houses at correspondingly higher prices; golf and ski package plans also available

Address:

P.O. Box 2499, Truckee, California 95734

Phone:

(916) 562-1111; toll free in California (800) 562-1113; toll free out of state (800) 824-8516

Typical Northstar architecture

Unlike most ski resorts, which rent land from the forest service, Northstar owns its property—2,500 acres of valley, forest, and mountain land—and it can decide for itself how it wants to develop it. So far, the pace has been slow and careful, with only seven percent of the land in use. Construction did not begin until the early 1970s, thus everything is relatively new, but already Northstar has established itself as one of California's major resorts, with a complete array of support facilities and recreational activities.

The focus of the resort is Northstar Village, located at the base of the downhill ski area, where a double and triple chair lift take off, carrying skiers to the mountaintop 2,200 feet above. The "village" is actually a long, rambling, modern structure, with shops and services on the ground level and lodging accommodations on the floors above. The condominiums and houses are clustered together around the village. Some of them are a distance away, but one of the advantages of Northstar is the free shuttle bus service that links the housing and recreational facilities with the central village, allowing guests to park their cars and forget them. The village has a delicatessen, a general store, a large ski and sports equipment shop, a tavern, and the Schaffer's Mill Restaurant and Bar. Just a short walk through the woods, across a small stream, is the recreational center, where the tennis courts and swimming pool are located.

It is a credit to Northstar (one that befits the tree-growing philosophy of its parent company, the Louisiana Pacific Corporation) that tree preservation has become a hallmark of the development. The condominiums, parking lots, and recreational areas are cleverly hidden among stands of pines and fir so that much of the construction is barely discernible in the natural setting.

Many of the condominiums, as well as the vacation houses on the property, are in the rental pool and available to the general public. Some are near the ski area; one group, for instance, is actually bisected by the double chair lift so that its occupants can strap on their skis at their front doors in the morning and sail down to be first in line. Some other condos are on the golf course and others are scattered along high ridges where they can take full advantage of commanding views.

In spite of the resort's self-contained nature, its easy proximity to the north end of Lake Tahoe and to Tahoe City is a welcome attraction to many visitors and serves to round out the spectrum of activities guests are able to enjoy.

Routes and Distances

From San Francisco and Sacramento take Interstate 80 east toward Reno. Cross Donner Pass and make a long descent to Truckee. On the far side of Truckee, look for a right turn onto the exit to Route 267. Follow 267 for six miles to the Northstar entrance sign. Turn right and the registration office will be seen immediately on the right. At the office you will be given your keys, a map of the complex, and instructions for getting to your accommodations, which will be anywhere within a mile of the office. All units have adequate parking directly adjacent.

Accommodations

With over a third of the 600 privately owned condominiums and houses in the rental pool, there is something at Northstar for just about everyone.

Right in the heart of the resort are two levels of "village unit" accommodations above the many little stores and shops along the mall. Thirty-seven rooms on the first level, referred to as "lodgettes," are basically hotel rooms, while each of the twenty-five deluxe "penthouse units" on the top level has a kitchen, a fireplace, and a spacious loft bedroom. One of the couches in the beautifully furnished living room converts into a queen-sized bed, making a penthouse unit a comfortable arrangement for four people. All of these village units have the advantage of being within a stone's throw of where the ski lifts take off and they are just as close to the tennis courts and pools in the recreation center.

The several outlying condominium clusters vary architecturally, but

Summer ride in high Sierras near Northstar

all feature an alpine design, with steep roofs and rough cedar siding, and are completely modern in their appointments. Accommodations in the condominiums range in size from modest studio apartments to four-bedroom, two-bath units. Some individual homes also are available, but these usually are rented on a weekly basis or longer.

A two-night minimum rental applies to all accommodations other than the individual homes.

Activities

With its choice location deep in the Sierras, Northstar is an all-year playground. To many, the winter ski program has become well known since the resort opened in 1972, but few realize that Northstar has just as much to offer during the summer months.

Of prime interest to summer vacationers is the championship golf course, the second nine of which just recently has been completed. With fairways winding through pine-forested hills and over the level terrain of the valley, the course is a challenge to the best, and the water hazards on fourteen of the holes do not make it any easier to score. Just recently, a new clubhouse also has been completed, with a full pro shop facility as well as excellent food service. If golf is your interest, you might want to request one of the condominiums along the edge of the course, although with the shuttle service, you can get there in no time from any point in Northstar.

The recreation center is another focus of activity in summertime. It is built around an Olympic-sized swimming pool, flanked on one side by a spacious deck for sunning and lounging and on the other by a twenty-five-foot Jacuzzi and a dressing room area. Ten beautifully kept Laykold tennis courts surround the pool complex and guests are allowed a generous

Winter scene in Northstar Village

amount of playing time without paying a fee. Circling the entire area and passing through a dense grove of aspen is a well-designed par course for those who are keeping fit.

The stable at Northstar is another on-site summer attraction. A string of around fifteen horses is brought in from Reno each season and an ambitious program that includes group and private lessons, guided tours through the Sierras, breakfast rides, moonlight rides, and overnight camp-outs has been popular with young and old alike.

When winter comes to the Sierras, Northstar has a program to match any of its rivals. Mount Pluto, its privately owned mountain, reaches an elevation of 8,600 feet and boasts excellent snow conditions for an exceptionally long season, running in a typical year from late November through April.

From Northstar Village two preliminary lifts carry skiers up to Big Springs Inn, a day lodge with restaurant, bar, and rest room facilities. From here lifts fan out all over the mountainside, transporting skiers to slopes ranging from beginning to expert on over a thousand acres of terrain.

One of the nice features of skiing Northstar is the management policy of limiting ski ticket sales to 5,500 per day, thus preventing interminable waits in the lift lines. (The limitation applies only to the general public, however; overnight guests can purchase tickets anytime at a special sales booth set aside for residents.)

Snow conditions permitting, Nordic skiing is also big at Northstar. The golf pro shop doubles as the Nordic center in winter and is well equipped with cross-country ski gear both for sale and for rent. There are forty kilometers of marked trails, twenty of which are machine groomed, through the golf course area. A minimal fee is assessed for using the trails. An expert staff provides lessons in Nordic technique and guided daytime and moonlight tours.

Whatever kind of skiing you prefer, the après-ski time is always a favorite finale. Start with a soak in the hot outdoor Jacuzzi, then join friends for beer or hot spiced wine at the Rendezvous Bar or the bar at Schaffer's Mill, both right in the center of the village.

If you have any residual energy after the day's activities and wish to pursue a bit of night life, the Cal-Neva Casino is just a few miles away. There, you can try your luck at almost any gambling game, and for just the time it takes to place a phone call, the management at the casino will send a courtesy car to pick you up, and also will deliver you back to your quarters again when the evening is over.

Dining

Not far from Northstar are Truckee, Tahoe City, Kings Beach, and other towns strung out along Lake Tahoe that boast any number of inter-esting restaurants. It would be remiss, however, not to start first with an evening at Northstar's own contribution to fine dining, Schaffer's Mill in the village.

Outside the entrance to this restaurant, which features old-time logging decor, a blackboard lists the specialties of the day, usually a nice selection of seafood, steak, and chicken entrées. Prices are moderate and the service friendly and helpful. Dinner is served between 5:30 and 9:30 daily, but no reservations are accepted, so a short wait sometimes is necessary. The time can be whiled away pleasantly enough in the adjacent Loggers Bar, which is adorned with old saws, logging tools, and photos from the period years ago when this was a logging camp. Lively entertainment is often available in the bar throughout the evening. Breakfast and lunch also are served at Schaffer's Mill, although should you prefer to eat in your quarters or take a picnic somewhere, supplies can be obtained at the deli and the general store.

For other options, Truckee is just six miles to the north. O.B.'s Board in the heart of the downtown section is highly recommended, as is The Passage, just across the street, in the venerable Truckee Hotel.

In the other direction, at Kings Beach, the Cantina Los Tres Hombres enjoys the reputation of having the best Mexican food on the lake, as well as being fun and having a friendly atmosphere. For something more formal, try La Cheminée, a fine restaurant featuring country French cooking.

At Tahoe Vista a little farther along, you will find a restaurant that is unprepossessing on the outside, but reputedly is the best on the lake; in fact, many people consider it to be one of the finest in California. This is Le Petit Pier, which serves "specialties of France" in a formal setting and, as you would expect, at somewhat dearer prices than those at other Tahoe restaurants. There are two seatings each evening, with reservations required, usually well in advance. Check the times when making a reservation.

Next door, the same ownership runs another popular dockside restaurant called Captain Jon's, which specializes in seafood dishes. Dinner here is served in a less formal atmosphere at more modest prices, but food preparation nevertheless is taken very seriously. This restaurant also requires a reservation and has just two seatings, at six and nine, which allows the chef to prepare the special sauces for which he is famous, and which he must do all at once and at just the proper time before they are to be served. Captain Jon's usually will have a number of specialties that do not appear on the menu, depending on what seafoods are particularly good and available at the time. Excellent homemade soup comes with the dinner here, as well as champagne sherbet to clear the palate between the soup and the fish courses. For those who dare, there is a final tempting selection of desserts.

The list of good restaurants could go on as there are at least two dozen close by, but those described here should provide a good start for new visitors to the area.

Cal-Neva Lodge

Distances:
> From San Francisco—206 miles; allow 4½ hours
>
> From Reno—48 miles; allow 1 hour

Features:
> Venerable casino-hotel astride the California-Nevada state line, over-looking north Lake Tahoe; offers comfort, entertainment, and plenty of indoor and outdoor sports

Activities:
> Gambling, exploring Tahoe's shops, restaurants, and natural attractions year around; tennis, golf, horseback riding, swimming in summer; cross-country and downhill skiing, snow-mobiling in winter

Seasons:
> Year around, twenty-four hours per day

Rates:
> Summer high season—$58 to $68 for two people in tower rooms, $53 to $125 in chalets (available only in summer); winter room rates—$38 midweek and $50 weekends

Address:
> Cal-Neva Lodge, P.O. Box 368, Crystal Bay, Nevada 89402

Phones:
> (702) 831-1511, or toll free (800) 648-4577

Entrance to Cal-Neva Lodge

To many an old-timer, the very mention of Cal-Neva makes the eyes twinkle and the mind fill with thoughts of glamour, excitement, celebrities, fun, and profit. The name has been associated with all this and more ever since it was first built in the 1920s and was the haunt of wealthy and discriminating San Franciscans and Angelenos, long before the big casinos as Las Vegas and Reno were ever dreamed of.

In the original old casino, the dance hall was on the state line and a painted stripe across the floor indicated whether you were dancing in California or Nevada. And if you were on the California side, all you had to do was step over the line to try your luck at the gaming equipment lining the walls on the Nevada side. (Today, the line still shows across the middle of the swimming pool outside the old building, so you can swim back and forth from state to state.)

Just like its habitues, Cal-Neva has been up and down on its luck over the years and has had a succession of owners, including Frank Sinatra, who was once the proprietor. The place burned to the ground in the 1930s, and people still talk about how it was completely rebuilt in the impossible time of thirty days to meet an essential commitment. But in spite of its volatile history, most of the changes over the years have brought improvements that have gradually added to Cal-Neva's attractions.

Upon checking in, you will discover that it is hard to find the registration desk, which is tucked away in an obscure corner. After that, it

Winter view of Cal-Neva's pool and famed circular bar

is even harder to find the elevators to your quarters because you must first thread your way right through the gaming room, bags in hand, past batteries of slot machines and blackjack tables.

But this is all part of the atmosphere, which is informal, unsophisticated, and full of good fun. It is considerably more relaxed and companionable than that of the glittering, polished casinos to the south and east. And it is notable that the smart set still loves Cal-Neva as much as always, except now when you see them, they are likely to be in jeans and cowboy hats, just blending into the general crowd.

Routes and Distances

From San Francisco and Sacramento take Interstate 80 toward Reno. Cross the 7,000-foot Donner Summit at Soda Springs (carry chains in winter). Then, drop down to Truckee and look for the junction with Route 267, which leads directly to Crystal Bay on the state line. Cal-Neva Lodge will be found right on the lake front, its tall tower making it easy to spot.

Accommodations

The relatively new tower addition (which clashes somewhat with the old construction) contains most of the 200 rooms here. Being new, these rooms are spacious and comfortable, and every one has a grand view of Lake Tahoe and the mountains beyond. The rooms are much alike, each with two queen-sized beds, a game table and chairs in front of a view window, a color television, and a big bathroom. Eighteen units have attached sitting rooms and therefore can be rented as suites.

In summertime only, the lodge also rents twenty-three chalets, scattered on the hillside below the tower, facing the lake. The chalets were once the major accommodations, but they are hard to heat and service in winter and have declined in importance. In the fine summer weather, however, they offer privacy and a sense of receiving "special treatment," which some old-timers still appreciate.

Upon checking into Cal-Neva, you either can trundle your own luggage up to the room or have a bellhop do it for you, leading the way past all the gamblers. If you have a chalet, however, the bellhop will be necessary, because you never will find your place on your own the first time.

Activities

The gaming never stops at Cal-Neva, and some people never seem to stop gaming. It is not unusual to come down for breakfast and find some of the same ones perched at the tables where you left them the night before. Blackjack and slots are the main diversions, but roulette, craps, bingo, and usually western-style poker also are played. If you hate to take time out for eating, keno cards are available at every table in the restaurant and each seat at the bar, so you can continue to play while taking nourishment. The famous circular bar is adjacent to the game room and looks out over the lake, though it is not necessary to pay for a drink when you are thirsty. Waitresses circulate constantly among the tables and slot machines taking orders for free drinks from the gamblers. (If they remember to tip, they do it by tossing a chip from the table onto a waitress' tray.)

The nice thing about Cal-Neva is that there also are lots of more vigorous activities in the vicinity, which sometimes can save you a bundle of money. Two tennis courts on the property, for instance, become popular as soon as the snow melts in the spring. The swimming pool, on a patio below the bar, opens up at about the same time. If the inn's own tennis courts get too crowded, you can use additional courts at a tennis club in Incline Village, with free transportation provided back and forth. Incline also has two eighteen-hole championship golf courses, both laid out by Robert Trent Jones and considered among the finest in California.

At any time of year it is fun to see the rest of the Lake Tahoe area. You can drive all the way around the lake, for example, in a couple of hours. (But be forewarned: the road is narrow, and to the south around Emerald Bay, which is the most beautiful part, it is snakelike and slow going. At the height of summer, the whole distance can become bumper-to-bumper traffic.)

One thing you will notice right away at Cal-Neva is the long row of locking ski racks at the front entrance. In winter, these are always in use,

Eighteen ski areas are near Cal-Neva

with streams of skiers coming and going at all times. The astounding fact is that there are eighteen ski areas within a half-hour distance. To take full advantage of the situation, the lodge employs a "ski host," who holds free clinics for guests in the evening, shows skiing movies (with complimentary wine and cheese), and advises about places to go and ski conditions in the area. A shuttle provides free transportation to the major areas, including Squaw Valley, Ski Incline, and Alpine Meadows, and it is possible to purchase special lift tickets that entitle you to ski at any of those places interchangeably. For cross-country people, there are good places to go at Incline, Donner Summit, and Ponderosa Ranch, which is located just around the bend of the lake past Incline Village. (You will remember Ponderosa Ranch as the setting for the famous television series "Bonanza.") Now, besides cross-country skiing, it offers snowmobiling in winter and horseback riding in summer. Either way, it provides an opportunity to get up into the hills behind the lake to see some interesting country.

Back at the lodge, after skiing or driving, a large spa-sauna-workout room is available to top off the day before the evening activity commences. Then, inevitably, it is down to the game room for some serious business.

Dining

The upper lake area of Tahoe is loaded with good places to dine. A few of the best are: The Carnelian House at Carnelian Bay, Schaffer's Mill at Northstar, The Tahoe House at Tahoe City, and Benissimo's Italian Restaurant next door in Kings Beach. Taking the tram up to Squaw Valley's High Camp for lunch is a breathtaking experience. There are many other places, too, and it is a good idea to go to the lodge's newsstand and pick up a copy of *The Guide,* which lists all the area's restaurants and has copies of their latest menus.

However, it is not really necessary to leave the lodge at all if you do not want to. Its Lake Room, which is open twenty-four hours a day, serves continental cuisine in a pleasant atmosphere and affords fine views over Tahoe. The Showroom offers buffet dining and entertainment, with tiers of tables arranged in a semicircle around a stage. The entertainment changes from time to time. When we were there it consisted of a country rock band and a bucking mechanical bull. Young hopefuls filed up to see if they could stay on for twenty seconds. Most failed, but those who succeeded always got a big hand. In between the rodeo exhibitions, couples drifted down to the floor to dance. The Showroom buffet is inexpensive, illustrated by the margaritas served for $2.50 for a half-carafe. The gambling, it seems, enables the management to offer other amenities at attractive prices. Perhaps the best buy of all is the traditional Sunday champagne brunch for $5.95, a delightful and fulsome repast, with as many champagne refills as you want.

Tahoe's
West Shore Condos

Distances:

From San Francisco—205 miles; allow 4 hours

From Reno—43 miles; allow 1 hour

Features:

A mile high in the middle of the Sierras where it gets much sunshine, Lake Tahoe is a natural center for recreation; its popular west shore has attracted a concentration of deluxe condominium developments, five of which are described here because they offer rentals to the public

Activities:

Tennis and swimming at all five condominiums; lake activities, skiing, golf, gambling, shopping, gallery browsing, hiking, river rafting, bicycling nearby

Seasons:

Year around

Rates:

Seasonal patterns vary from year to year and rates are changeable. In general, however, there are three seasons: the off season (spring and late fall), with rates from $37.50 to $75 for two people; the summer season, with rates from $45 to $110; and the ski season, with rates from $65 to $115; the low rates are for single bedrooms, the high rates for multi-room condos

Addresses and Phones:

Tahoe Tavern, Box 82, Tahoe City, California 95730
(916) 583-3704

Granlibakken, P.O. Box 6329, Tahoe City, California 95730
(916) 583-4242

Rocky Ridge, 1877 Northlake Boulevard, Tahoe City, California 95730
(916) 583-3723

Chinquapin, P.O. Box RR, Tahoe City, California 95730
(916) 583-6991

Carnelian Woods, P.O. Box 62, Carnelian Bay, California 95711
(916) 546-5924

Tahoe Tavern is located on waterfront

The focal point of Tahoe's west shore, Tahoe City is a small town by city standards, but aside from South Lake Tahoe, is the biggest town on the lake. It therefore has enough shops to supply almost every need. It is replete with good restaurants offering a wide variety of menus, interesting boutiques and galleries for browsing, and its central location places it within easy range of all the attractions of the whole Tahoe region. Squaw

Valley and Alpine Meadows, for instance, are only ten minutes away, the Nevada casinos not more than twenty, and the boating and water sports afforded by the lake itself are on its very doorstep.

It is no wonder that condominium developers picked this particular area for concentrating their efforts, and the result has been that well over a dozen elegant condo projects, of all sizes and shapes, have sprung up along the west shore. Five of the best of these have active rental programs and are particularly well situated to promise the most fun on a Lake Tahoe getaway.

Routes and Distances

From San Francisco and Sacramento take Interstate 80 east across Donner Summit to Truckee. At Truckee turn south on Highway 89 to Tahoe City. Look for some fine early views of beautiful Lake Tahoe at the point where 89 begins its descent.

Four of the five condominiums are in Tahoe City. To get to the first one, Tahoe Tavern, turn right at Fanny Bridge upon entering Tahoe City, and you will bc on West Lake Boulevard. Not more than a quarter mile to the south on West Lake, on the lake side, you will see the Tahoe Tavern-Tahoe Shores entrance sign.

To get to Granlibakken, go exactly the same way, but at the Tahoe Tavern sign, turn right instead of left and go a half mile up Tonopah Avenue to the Granlibakken entrance.

Rocky Ridge is on the north edge of town, just a few hundred yards

Granlibakken has its own ski area

past the last stores as you head up Highway 28. The Rocky Ridge Road is plainly marked and the rental office, where you check in, is on the corner.

Another two miles up Highway 28 is Chinquapin, which is on the lake side of the road, and is well marked with a large sign. At Carnelian Bay, 2.7 miles farther, is the turnoff to the Carnelian Woods condominiums, located to the left, only a half block from the center of the little town.

Accommodations

Besides its full-size condominiums, Granlibakken has one building made up wholly of suites, each of which consists of a living room and kitchen combination called a studio and an adjoining bedroom. Because the studio and the bedroom have separate baths and separate entrances and the studio has a hide-a-bed sofa, a suite can be rented as an expansive and comfortable whole, or divided into two parts and rented separately. (The studio also has a fireplace.) Granlibakken is the only one of the condos with such an arrangement. Being the smallest quarters available, they account for the lowest range of rates available for these five condominiums.

Other than Granlibakken's suites, accommodations at all five developments are typical second-home condos, ranging from one to five bedrooms in size, with full kitchens, dining areas, outside decks, and laundry facilities; every comfort and convenience, in other words, that would be expected in a regular home. Being individually owned and

Rocky Ridge condos

furnished, no two units are the same, even within any one complex, but all are relatively new, modern, and unquestionably the most comfortable vacation accommodations in the neighborhood.

The size of the bigger condominiums renders them especially ideal for families, or for two couples to share. At Rocky Ridge, for instance, where the smallest unit has three bedrooms, the most expensive ones with magnificent sweeping views of the whole lake, rent for $625 per week. For two couples sharing these units, the cost is only $45 per day per couple, no more than they might pay for a single motel room. But for the money, they get several times as much space and privacy, plus the convenience (and savings potential) of having their own kitchen to prepare meals when they don't feel like going out.

Activities

All of these condominiums have their own tennis facilities and swimming pools, and some of them have additional amenities besides.

Tahoe Tavern has eight courts and two pools, one at each end of the long complex. Built on the waterfront, Tahoe Tavern also offers lake swimming and water sports in summer, with two long piers to facilitate these activities.

Granlibakken has six tennis courts, with a nice swimming pool above them on the hillside next to the main administration building. In winter, the pool is closed, but a large hot spa, much in favor with skiers, is kept

Chinquapin condos overlook Lake Tahoe

Carnelian Woods recreation center

operating all year around. Granlibakken has the distinction of operating its own ski area right behind the condominiums. Though not very big—it has just two tows, a poma lift and a rope—it is a fine practice slope and very popular, especially with younger skiers. Best of all, guests pay no charge for its use.

Rocky Ridge boasts a spectacular free-form pool set on the edge of the rimrock, where it has a sweeping view of the whole lake from a pretty trellised deck. In the center of the property are four tennis courts and a small pro shop. In order to obtain its tremendous vistas, Rocky Ridge was built on high ground back from the lake, but it also has its own private beach, with a lodge and dressing rooms, on the lake only a few minutes' drive away.

At Chinquapin, six tennis courts are grouped on one side of a club-house in the center of the complex, with a swimming pool built into a deck on the opposite side. At the south end, built out over the lake on a little spit, is a seventh court, all by itself. Chinquapin, occupying a good thousand feet of lakefront, also sports a long boat dock with buoy tie-ups for several dozen boats and, of course, offers fine lake swimming.

Carnelian Woods has three tennis courts and one of the handsomest swimming pools we have seen, located in a wooded site behind the recreation buiding. There is also a one-mile par course for jogging and a big outdoor whirlpool Jacuzzi. Although the condominiums are not on the lake itself, guests at Carnelian Woods have beach privileges at Club Innisfree, about a quarter mile down the road.

All told, there are twenty-eight tennis courts in these five complexes and, to their credit, every one of them is properly surfaced and fenced, kept in top condition, and available to guests without cost.

In winter, these condominiums are used heavily on weekends and holidays by skiers who check in on Friday night, ski Saturday and Sunday, and return home Sunday evening. They have a choice of a dozen good ski areas, but tend to favor Alpine Meadows and Squaw Valley because both are so close.

When the snow is off the ground, beginning about April, golfers can play the two excellent eighteen-hole courses at Incline Village, a half hour away, or the new eighteen-hole championship course at Northstar. There are also two nine-hole courses nearby, one in Tahoe City and the other at Brockway, two miles past Carnelian Bay near Kings Beach.

Two sports that have been growing in popularity are bicycling and river rafting. Rafts can be rented at Truckee River Raft Rentals Company, and both bikes and rafts are available at the High Wheeler Rental Company. Or come prepared by bringing your own equipment. Tahoe City also has a number of boat rental places for sailboats, canoes, kayaks, and fishing boats. The fishing is often good both on the lake and in the river, and any fisherman can set his juices flowing by going out to stand for awhile on Fanny Bridge in downtown Tahoe City. Right below this bridge there are always schools of big trout that strike hungrily at any morsels tossed to them. The nickname "Fanny Bridge," of course, stems from the line of derrieres exposed to view when everyone is hanging over the rail watching the fish.

Tahoe City has an active and helpful visitors' bureau attached to the chamber of commerce, and a visit to the office in the rear of the Lighthouse Shopping Center will elicit a wealth of information about all the other specific things to explore in the area, such as hiking trails, Nordic skiing, and points of interest.

All of the activities discussed so far are, of course, for daytime. In the evening the activity moves around the end of the lake to the Nevada casinos, twenty minutes away, where, with skill and a little luck, you can earn back whatever costs were incurred by the day's fun.

Dining

All of the condos have modern kitchens, but you probably will not want to eat in all the time, at least for dinner, so it is good to know that there are plenty of enticing options in the neighborhood.

In Tahoe City alone, there are a number of places within walking distance of each other, right on the lake. They all are so good that choosing among them is a problem. Just below the Lighthouse Shopping

Center, for instance, two new buildings of wooden open beam construction hug the shoreline of the lake. Each contains an interesting restaurant, with walls of glass along the view side. One of these, The Chart House, has a fine view of the lake and mountains as well as a fascinating interior featuring a display of authentic naval antiques and relics. It also has an excellent menu and is especially noted for its salad bar. Next door is Jake's on the Lake, whose bar is the hands-down favorite with locals and visitors alike. Nor does the restaurant lag much behind in popularity. The key location is given to the bar, where intimate furniture groupings along the windows overlooking the lake make a romantic spot for enjoying a cocktail at the end of the day. The restaurant is informal and features good seafood, chicken, and steak dinners for modest prices. Luncheon is served in summertime on the deck overlooking a large fleet of sailboats.

Tomfoolery is another restaurant with a distinct personality, where you can dine on what the management proclaims to be "fanciful food and spirits." The house specialties are fondues (though other choices are available) and each table is outfitted with a heating apparatus for fondue cookery. A good approach for two people is for one to order the seafood selection, which includes fish, lobster, prawns, scallops, and raw vegetables, while the other orders lean beef chunks. Since everything is cooked in the same oil and both orders are served with a fascinating selection of condiments, sharing this array and cooking it on the bamboo skewers provided makes an interesting evening. Part of the fun is that at no time are you offered eating utensils. The first course of thick homemade soup is ladled into crockery cups for drinking, and the garden salad is made of raw vegetables, which must be eaten with the fingers.

Next door to Tomfoolery is an informal Mexican restaurant, Los Tres Hombres Taco City, an offshoot of the Cantina Los Tres Hombres in Kings Beach, specializing in homemade food guaranteed to titillate afficionados of genuine Mexican fare. Other fine ethnic restaurants in town are Bacchi's Inn, which has been serving fine Italian food for over fifty years, on Lake Forest Road, and the Pfeifer House, which is just west of Tahoe City on Highway 89 and is known for authentic German cuisine. A new restaurant just a mile south of town, The Tahoe House, features good Swiss food, with the recipes brought from Zurich by the owner-chef. Veal fans should look no farther. The Carnelian House, along the north shore, deserves special mention because it not only has a reputation for fine continental cuisine and a superlative view of the lake, but also is located just across the road from the Carnelian Woods condominiums.

These Tahoe City restaurants are just a smattering of what is available along the lake. For a few suggestions farther up on the north shore, twenty minutes away, check the chapters on Northstar and Cal-Neva.

Lakeland Village
Beach and Ski Resort

Distances:

> From San Francisco—185 miles; allow 3½ hours
> From Los Angeles—414 miles; allow 9 hours

Features:

> A large, compactly arranged condominium development; located on Tahoe's south shore, close to the Nevada state line; area boasts eighty percent chance of sunshine year around

Activities:

> Downhill and cross-country skiing, swimming, tennis, golf, hiking, boating, fishing, and other water activities; casino entertainment and gambling five minutes away

Seasons:

> Year around; high season—mid-June through mid-September and all holidays; ski season—4 January through late April; low season— mid-September to Christmas and late April through mid-June

Rates:

> For two people, $59 to $125 for high season, $55 to $120 for ski season, $45 to $88 for low season

Address:

> P.O. Box A, South Lake Tahoe, California 95705

Phone:

> (916) 541-7711, or toll free in California (800) 822-5969

Lakeland condos line Lake Tahoe

Lakeland Village Beach and Ski Resort is aptly named. Its nineteen acres of pine-forested land front on a thousand feet of level, sandy Lake Tahoe beach, and the runs of the big Heavenly Valley ski area can be seen clearly on the mountainside just a mile away. And, for those not familiar with Heavenly Valley, this is no ordinary ski area. It spreads into two states, with twenty-six lifts taking skiers up to nine peaks and literally hundreds of runs. The top elevation of the Heavenly Nevada run is 10,100 feet, and Heavenly California is 10,040 feet, with trails connecting the two for those inclined to interstate skiing. In late spring, when there is little snow to be seen at Heavenly's base lodge, there nevertheless is plenty on top, so that skiers can have the best of two worlds. Those who come back early to their house in the village will find sunshine still warming the tennis courts, the beach, and the swimming pools.

Lakeland unquestionably offers as comfortable and convenient ski quarters as can be found anywhere. All the units are privately owned and furnished condominiums, about two hundred of which are maintained in a rental pool available to the general public. And like most such developments, these privately owned quarters invariably tend to be spacious, tastefully furnished, and full of the niceties that make it fun to live away from home now and then.

Lakeland Village does not have its own restaurant, but that does not matter because the area is loaded with good places to eat. On the other hand, it does, because of its advantageous position at the very southern end of the lake, allow easy access to all of Tahoe's many other attractions, not the least of which is the freewheeling night life just minutes away at Stateline.

Routes and Distances

From San Francisco take Interstate 80 to Sacramento, then U.S. 50 from there east through Placerville and Kyburz all the way to South Lake Tahoe. Strung out on the highway, this is a long town, with a lot of commercial activity and motels. At the point where the highway gets closest to the lake, about a mile and a quarter from the state line, Lakeland Village's condominiums and entrance portal will be seen on the left.

Accommodations

There are ten different sized condominiums in this development, ranging from one-room studios to four-bedroom, three-bath townhouses. The studios take two people, while the largest townhouses hold up to ten, with every size in between.

Each unit, large or small, has its own fireplace (some are gas and some are woodburning), a furnished private deck, color television, and a large, fully equipped kitchen and dining arrangement. There is plenty of closet and storage space and comfortable furniture. The fact that these really are, in effect, people's homes explains the cozy, homelike atmosphere.

Because of the complexity of the seasonal patterns here and the many different sized units, it is worthwhile to call ahead early and discuss your plans with the reservations department. Package plans, which change from time to time, are often available for both skiers and gamblers, so these, too, should be explored.

The atmosphere at Lakeland Village is informal. When you first arrive, bell service is available to help you move into your unit, but it is not mandatory. There is plenty of parking space close to all the units and, in the morning, a free copy of the San Francisco newspaper can be picked up at the front desk.

Activities

Skiing, of course, is the main activity in wintertime, excluding momentarily the gambling activities across the line. Besides Heavenly Valley right next door, and Kirkwood in the mountains thirty miles to the south, there is a whole chain of ski areas within easy access from the highway on the west and north sides of the lake. Here is how some of the major areas rate themselves. Heavenly Valley is the highest, with 4,000 feet of vertical drop, and twenty-five percent of its runs are for advanced skiers. Alpine Meadows has 1,700 feet of drop, thirteen lifts, and forty

Even in winter sun worshipers like Lakeland Village's beach

percent advanced runs. Ski Incline is 900 feet high, with seven lifts and twenty percent advanced runs. Squaw Valley rises 2,700 feet, and has twenty-six lifts and twenty percent advanced runs. A number of these ski areas run shuttle bus services of one kind or another to the lodging facilities in South Lake Tahoe. Ask at the front desk about the schedules.

There also are at least eight Nordic ski areas with groomed and marked trails, and more open each year as cross-country skiing continues to gain in popularity. Zepher Cove Nordic Company is the closest, just around the lake to the east on the Nevada side, and both Kirkwood and Squaw Valley have groomed trails and offer instruction. The biggest Nordic operation, however, is at Royal Gorge near Donner Summit, with 125 miles of trails of all degrees of difficulty.

By April or May, the emphasis begins to shift to summer sports. There are two heated swimming pools on the property (one of which is kept open all year, making it an après-ski favorite) and, of course, there is the long, private sand beach on the lake. Two excellent hard-surfaced tennis courts are available for a nominal fee. Golfers go to the closest course, the eighteen-hole Lake Tahoe Country Club near the South Lake Tahoe airport, or they go to Brockway, or, better still, to Incline Village with its two superb eighteen-hole courses.

There is a large hot spa next to the year-round pool, as well as volleyball, Ping Pong, croquet, horseshoes, and miscellaneous other diversions available along with paddle boats, canoes, inner tubes, and surf-riders for rent at the beach. The lake offers good trout fishing all year around. There are bicycle trails in the vicinity, and no end of hiking opportunities in the state parks bordering the west side of the lake and in the Desolation Wilderness off Highway 89.

For beautiful scenery, take the short drive up the west side of the lake to Emerald Bay, said to be one of the most photographed scenes in the world. In summertime, a one-mile trail from the Emerald Bay overlook leads down to the remarkable thirty-eight-room Vikingsholm, a reproduction of an ancient Scandinavian castle-fortress built in 1929 by an eccentric heiress, Mrs. Lora Knight. Then, if you have not already been there to ski, continue on around the lake to visit Squaw Valley and see where the 1960 Winter Olympics were held. A ride up the tramway (six dollars for nonskiers) is an experience to remember. After that, proceed to Tahoe City, known as the hub of the west shore, and look at the sights. One of these is Fanny Bridge, where highways 89 and 28 converge over the Truckee River, and where people crowd around to look at the fat trout congregated in the clear waters below.

Lakeland Village maintains an activities director to help guests with arrangements and schedules for all of these many things to do. In the evening, however, no one needs help with the big attractions, the nearby casinos. The village provides free shuttle service for the five-minute trip (just ask at the desk). Three major casinos—Harrah's, Caesar's Palace,

Casinos are only minutes away from Lakeland Village

and the Sahara Tahoe—are clustered together, as close to the state line as they can get, with some smaller places nestled in between. The little casinos concentrate mostly on gambling, but the big three, with huge gaming rooms, also have lavish exhibits, floor shows, and a constant succession of big-name entertainment. Everything on this side of the border operates twenty-four hours a day, seven days a week, and if you do not come home a winner, it can't be blamed on lack of opportunity.

Dining

With a good kitchen in every unit, you can dine "at home" if you like. If you choose instead to dine out, there are lots of places to go, some conveniently within walking distance. For breakfast, for instance, Heidis, which advertises "the best breakfast you'll ever have," is right next door. Belgian waffles, crepes, and fluffy four-egg omelettes are their specialties. Also in the neighborhood are the Cantina Los Tres Hombres for authentic Mexican cookery; the Chez Villaret, considered tops for gourmet French food; Dory's Oar, featuring New England–style seafood; and The Mine Shaft, which specializes in prime beef. These all are good choices, and for something light at any time of day, there is The Cookbook, "the home of 500 omelettes."

For glamour, the places to go are across the line in the Nevada casinos. The big ones all have two or more restaurants and prices are not expensive because the casinos try to attract people, thinking that once they are there they will drop a little money at the gaming tables. In the top of Harrah's, for instance, you will find The Summit, an elegant glass-enclosed gourmet restaurant with a panoramic view of Lake Tahoe and the mountains beyond. Also high in the tower is The Forest, one of the most lavish buffets you will experience anywhere. The inside of this big room is decorated to look like a forest grotto—full of flowers, rocks, and foliage—and offering a wide selection of tastily prepared food. For those in a hurry to get back to the tables, Harrah's Skyway Restaurant offers rapid buffet service and low prices.

Caesar's Palace has its Edgewood Room, another elegant dinner house, and the Sahara Tahoe has The House of Lords, a very plush restaurant that caters, as they put it, to "the extravagant tastes in all of us."

One final note about the serious business of eating in the glamorous casinos: some people are known to spend the whole night at the tables and find themselves, at dawn, down to a somewhat attenuated pile of chips. But to accommodate these unfortunates (and to the advantage of everyone else) the casino restaurants advertise "breakfast for 99¢" on neon signs out in the street. Maybe it is all intended just to lure people back to the slots inside, but these are the best breakfasts for the money you will find for a long time.

Strawberry Lodge

Distances:

From San Francisco—165 miles; allow 3½ hours
From Sacramento—80 miles; allow 1½ hours
From South Lake Tahoe—15 miles; allow ½ hour

Features:

A captivating getaway on a mountain stream in the high Sierras; filled with antiques and the promise of old-time fun and friendliness

Activities:

Tennis, swimming, horseback riding, hiking in summer; cross-country and downhill skiing in winter; "hot tubbing," Saturday night dancing, Wednesday night movies, technical rock climbing for experts, shopping for antiques, fishing

Seasons:

Year around

Rates:

$18 for two and $26 for four people in a skiers' bunk room; $25 for two people in a room with shared bath, $35 with bath; $35 for two people in motel room in annex; $50 for honeymoon room

Address:

Highway 50, Kyburz, California 95720

Phone:

(916) 659-7200

Lover's Leap looms behind Strawberry Lodge

Strawberry Lodge is a getaway in the true sense of the word. Located deep within the pristine and beautiful Sierras, this cozy retreat nevertheless is only a relatively short drive from several of California's main population centers. It is delightful to visit, even if you just spend an hour or so poking around in the big antique- and memento-filled area of the lodge's ground floor. Antique buffs will be especially interested because the owners have assembled a wide assortment of good pieces, most of which are for sale. Everyone else will just enjoy looking at the mementos, absorbing the atmosphere reminiscent of times past.

The site of Strawberry Lodge, at the head of Strawberry Canyon, has long been a major stopover for travelers crossing the Sierra Nevadas. It lies at the beginning of the long, high pass separating central California from the Lake Tahoe–Nevada territory. In the days of the great Nevada silver rush, Strawberry Station, as it was called then, was where the wagon trains and stages prepared themselves for the hard uphill pull ahead, or paused to rest after crossing the pass on the return trip. The station eventually grew into a small hotel, which in turn evolved into the present structure. It continued to cater quietly to travelers until sometime in the 1950s, when it suddenly captured the fancy of fashionable people from San Francisco and Sacramento and became notorious, for a time, as a very posh watering hole.

Then, with the 1960 Olympics and the subsequent rapid development of Lake Tahoe, everything changed; the action moved east and Strawberry

Lodge drifted downhill into disregard and neglect. It went through a long period of changing ownership and indifferent management until just two years ago, when an innovative pair of female entrepreneurs saw an opportunity to capitalize on the old inn's historical charm and unmatchable location. They suspected, too, that the glitter and superficiality of the newer resorts were beginning to wear thin, and people were ready to appreciate older, friendlier values.

These two felt they could rebuild those values at Strawberry, and they set about it with energy and imagination. In the two-year period, things changed fast, with recarpeting, redecorating, and refurnishing. A cross-country ski program was set up, the tennis courts resurfaced, a corral built, and a string of saddle horses acquired. Then a chef was chosen and trained to create the best kitchen between Sacramento and Tahoe.

Bonny Madsen and Kim Peterson have now become well-known characters in the valley, where the local people, who remember the lodge's days of questionable reputation, laughingly refer to them as the "shady ladies of Strawberry." Anyone who remembers the place from twenty-five years back will be thrilled with the remarkable job they have done to recreate the friendly, comfortable qualities of the old inn, while unobtrusively broadening and adding to the recreational facilities.

Routes and Distances

From anywhere in California, drive first to Sacramento, then take U.S. 50 eastbound. From Sacramento it is forty-two miles to Placerville, the historic jumping-off place for the California gold rush and later for the Nevada silver rush. Continue on 50 uphill to the little town of Kyburz. Nine miles past Kyburz, look for Strawberry Lodge on the right side of the highway, where it stands prominently alone.

Accommodations

During the extensive restoration, a great deal of attention has been devoted to the guest quarters on the second level of the lodge. One by one these upstairs rooms have been upgraded with fresh paint, tasteful wallpaper, and new drapes and bedspreads. Also, interesting antique furniture gradually is being acquired for all of the bedrooms. Of the seventeen rooms, ten have private baths. The other seven, in the tradition of so many of the early hostelries, share baths down the hall, although each room has a washstand.

With the exception of two expansive "honeymoon rooms," these guest quarters are fairly small, with little room for lounging, but this is of no concern since guests can use the big, cozy living room downstairs. Filled with comfortable, overstuffed furniture grouped around a huge fireplace, this lounge area is the focal point for good conversation with other guests enjoying the same relaxing atmosphere.

Besides the guest quarters in the lodge, thirteen additional rooms are available in the annex across the street. Also recently renovated, they help accommodate the overflow as Strawberry's popularity continues to grow.

Finally, in the lower level of the lodge, next to the ski shop, are some additional rooms. Built for use in a children's summer camping program, they are really very plain dormitory bunk rooms, but are worth mentioning because they are available at low prices in the winter for skiers and ski groups who want to save money for good food and lift tickets.

Activities

In winter, many people come to Strawberry just to sit before the big fireplace and watch the snow outside. This, however, does not reflect on the quality of the activities outside. The lodge has an excellent ski touring program run by a certified ski instructor, and there are over ten miles of marked and groomed cross-country ski trails emanating right from the lodge's front door. Complementing this program, on the lower level of the building, is a complete ski shop with both sales and rental equipment.

Excellent downhill skiing is just five miles away. Heading east on Highway 50, turn off at the well-marked "Pow Wow" sign to get to the Sierra Ski Ranch, a delightful low-keyed area with eight chair lifts and no long lines. A couple of day lodges with food service, ski school instruction, and a fully equipped ski shop contribute to making this a particularly pleasant place to ski.

Returning to Strawberry Lodge, you will find its bar is the local après-ski center, filled with both Nordic and alpine skiers who enjoy congregating and relaxing there before taking off for home.

This same bar is also a popular gathering spot on Wednesday nights when recent movies are shown on a big video screen, and also on Saturday evenings when dances with live music always attract a crowd to the big ballroom off the bar. Featuring country and western as well as rock bands, these Saturday events are enjoyed by both the local population and lodge guests.

In summer the swimming pool and tennis court become the focus of activity, and the hot tub continues to be an attraction, just as it was in winter. Around Memorial Day the lodge's fourteen horses are brought back from their winter pasture in Placerville. Then there are guided trail rides into the high Sierras and overnight trips and camp-outs, all easily planned with just a little advance notice.

For those who would rather walk there are hiking trails in every direction. The top of Lover's Leap, the gigantic rock formation behind the lodge across the river, is a favorite destination. Hikers approach it from the back side, leaving the face, one of the most challenging vertical walls in California, to expert rock climbers.

Several pretty alpine lakes, two of which are Cody Lake and Wright Lake, make nice hiking destinations from the lodge. Another particularly lovely one-day outing is a walk through the Desolation Wilderness, with

Ski touring group comes through the woods

Horse Tail Falls as the objective.

The south fork of the American River runs behind Strawberry Lodge, forming the border of the property as well as enhancing the beauty of the setting. Fly fishermen find this an enticing stream in which to challenge the wily trout, while adventurous types enjoy riding its current in inner tubes in the summer when the water warms up.

Dining

Strawberry's dining room opens off one side of the lounge area, and, like the rest of the lodge, has a rustic theme. A big stone fireplace dominates one end of the room and ox-yoke light fixtures hang from the dark open beam ceiling. The other walls of the room are ringed with antique chests and sideboards (all for sale) and cluttered with old-time bric-a-brac from the "station" days.

Opening off another side of the lounge is the saloon, a long narrow room dominated by an old carved wooden bar and heated by a big iron stove radiating cheer in the winter to skiers. The walls and even the ceiling of this room are almost completely papered with autographed dollar bills and cards left by hundreds of enthusiastic patrons. Charmaine, the bartender, is fondly known all up and down Highway 50. Her elaborate strawberry daiquiris are special favorites.

The chef, also a woman, runs a good kitchen and has a reputation for turning out reliably excellent food at reasonable prices. For example, a typical dinner for under ten dollars includes a good cream of asparagus soup, a crisp salad with eight vegetable ingredients, an entrée such as Shrimp Mornay or roast prime rib of beef, strawberry shortcake, and coffee. That's hard to beat for the money these days.

The restaurant is open seven days a week for all three meals. On Friday and Saturday evenings, and also during the popular Sunday brunch, live music to dine by is an added attraction.

Bear Valley Village

Distances:
From San Francisco—205 miles; allow 4 hours
From Sacramento—120 miles; allow 2½ hours

Features:
A complete, fully equipped destination resort located in a national forest bordering on a wilderness; best known to California skiers for Mount Reba's short lift lines and fine powder snow

Activities:
Cross-country and downhill skiing, "hot tubbing," après-ski entertainment in winter; swimming, sailing, bicycling, tennis, hiking, fishing, backpacking in summer

Seasons:
The ski season normally starts in November and runs through April, or even May; activities cease for the spring melt, then the summer season starts in late June or July and usually continues well into October

Rates:
Lodge rooms—$35 to $44 for two people; condominiums—from $58 for a studio up to $131 for the largest units, which sleep eight

Address:
Box 8, Bear Valley, California 95223

Phone:
Central Reservations—(209) 753-2311
Red Dog Lodge—(209) 753-2344

Bear Valley condominiums

Either by chance or design, Bear Valley seems to combine the best qualities of many of the outstanding Sierra resorts. Because it was developed later than most, it perhaps was able to learn from their accumulated experience and take advantage of it.

First, however, Bear Valley has the advantage of having a unique location deep within the Stanislaus National Forest, but also right adjacent to a designated wilderness, an area unmatched in pristine loveliness. About fifteen years ago, in what turned out to be a bit of luck, a rare parcel of privately owned property within the forest became available and was purchased by the farsighted people who envisioned the present Bear Valley development.

Surprisingly, the very fact that the property has finite boundaries, with no capacity for expanding into the forest, proved to be an advantage because knowing just what they had to work with forced the developers to design the community carefully. The pleasant result is that everything in the village—the lodges, condominiums, restaurants, bars, and a variety of interesting shops—is compactly arranged and within easy walking distance of each other.

Another circumstance that adds immeasurably to the charm of Bear Valley during the winter is that its fabulous Mount Reba ski area, which attracts skiers from all over central California, is four miles beyond the village. This means that all the milling traffic and overflowing parking lots that characterize most ski areas are far enough away to leave Bear Valley Village peaceful and undisturbed. Guests staying in the village usually park their cars when they arrive and forget them. From then on they take the convenient shuttle bus back and forth to the ski area and avoid traffic hassles. (Leaving the car too long in this part of the Sierras has just one disadvantage: it sometimes is necessary to hunt down the car and dig it out when it is time to go home.)

When the sun melts the blanket of snow from the many tiny alpine lakes and coaxes a host of wild flowers into making a colorful appearance on the forest floor, you can't help but wonder if this isn't the loveliest time of all in Bear Valley. The people who live here year around will confide that this certainly is true, and in the same breath, that they are greatly surprised how, with dry mountain air and temperatures averaging seventy-five degrees, summer fun in Bear Valley is still so undiscovered.

Routes and Distances

For San Franciscans the most direct route to Bear Valley is to take I-580 to I-205, then I-205 to the junction with I-5, and I-5 a very short distance to Route 120, which crosses to Manteca. At Manteca go north on Highway 99 for eleven miles to Route 4, which you then follow all the way to Bear Valley.

From Sacramento take Highway 16 to where it forms a junction with the "Mother Lode Highway," Highway 49. Follow 49 south through the

Bear Valley's Red Dog Lodge is a European-style hostelry

beautiful rolling green hills of the gold country to Angels Camp, where you pick up Route 4. From the junction it is approximately thirty-five miles on Route 4 to Bear Valley. The latter part of Route 4, past the town of Arnold, is a beautiful scenic drive.

Northeast of Bear Valley the road rises sharply to over nine thousand feet. It is impossible to keep this high area plowed in winter, at which time Bear Valley is approachable from only the west. For several months after July, however, you can get in from either side.

A word of warning: California, the Bear Flag state, loves bears and has at least three areas called Bear Valley, as well as Grizzly Flats. Be sure to go to the right Bear Valley on Highway 4.

Accommodations

The two types of accommodations available in Bear Valley Village are lodge rooms and condominiums. The rooms, at Red Dog Lodge, are very simple, laid out in the European hostelry style, and especially popular with skiers who just want a place to sleep. Most of Red Dog's rooms have one double and two single beds, with a chest of drawers and one chair. Plenty of towels hang on a rack in the room, but the men's and ladies' bathrooms are down the hall. (Those who remember Bear Valley from the past and stayed at the main lodge will wonder why its hotel rooms are not mentioned here. It is because they are being converted into miniature time-share condominiums and may no longer be available for rent, depending on the whims of the still unknown new owners. Only time will tell.)

The regular condominiums are the preferred places to stay as they are the most comfortable. They are located in four complexes scattered around the circle formed by the village road, and there are more being built, so the supply of rental units will continue to increase. The condos range from small studios that sleep two, to one-bedroom, two-bedroom, and three-bedroom models. Almost all of the latter have a hide-a-bed sofa in the living room so they can sleep anywhere from four to eight people. All but one of the condo layouts have kitchens or kitchenettes, and most, but not all, have fireplaces.

A nice thing about Bear Valley Village is that it has a completely stocked old-fashioned general store where you can pick up everything needed for your kitchen, plus most other incidentals you might need, from film to liquor to snow shovels. If the general store does not have what you want, Bear Valley's year-round sports shop probably will. There is also a coin-operated laundry and a gasoline station to round out the amenities.

Activities

Although it is known as a winter resort, Bear Valley is cranking up its summer programs and deserves, and undoubtedly will achieve, a great deal more summertime popularity than it currently enjoys. Spring comes late at

Summer bike race at Bear Valley

this altitude, but when it does, sometime in July, it comes in a rush. Then for four months the skies clear and the weather and outdoor living conditions are utterly beautiful.

Compared with the heat of California's central valleys, temperatures here are mild, perfect for tennis. Felix Barbera, the tennis professional, runs the summer program, with six tournament-quality, hard-surfaced courts to work on. They are seldom crowded, so Bear Valley is a good place either to play for fun or take lessons and brush up on your game.

Light traffic on the roads and the moderate temperatures are also good for bicyclists. Recreational riders take the flat roads along the valley floor, while serious riders go up the hill to Mount Reba and beyond. You must, however, bring your own bike as no rentals are available.

You also must bring your own boat for sailing. Lake Alpine, four miles up the road, is a beautiful mountain lake that has good breezes and is big enough for small craft, such as Lasers and Hobie cats. A public ramp is provided for easy launching. Lake Alpine is a favorite for swimming, too, at least for those who like brisk water, and has a nice beach. The lake is stocked regularly with trout and is considered a good producer by fishermen, who also can wet a line in the Stanislaus and other neighboring streams and high lakes.

The other summer activities are hiking and backpacking in the Stanislaus National Forest and in the Mokelumne Wilderness Area, adjoining Bear Valley, and, of course, swimming and sunning at Bear Valley's own heated pool.

An unusual event that takes place every summer in late July or August is "Music from Bear Valley," a two-week smorgasbord of light opera and classical music held outdoors or under canvas in the meadow. It is something that every music lover will thoroughly enjoy.

With the season's first snow, things change radically and Bear Valley reverts to what it is best known for: its uncrowded, relaxed ski resort

Bear Valley shuttle takes skiers to Mount Reba

facilities and generally good snow conditions. Mount Reba has seven chairs, the longest with 4,200 feet of vertical rise and the steepest with 1,300 feet. The area has a lodge with a cafeteria, snack bars, and the Bear Paw bar. The best way to ski Mount Reba, for guests at the valley, is to take the one-dollar shuttle bus to the mountain, ski as long as desired, and then make the final run of the day on the long Home Run, which follows a series of ridges all the way back to Bear Valley Lodge.

Cross-country skiers have two options. There is a regular Nordic ski center just across the highway that maintains thirty kilometers of double-tracked groomed trails. All-day passes cost three dollars and instruction is available. The other way to go is to tour the roads in the residential area north of Bear Valley Village. There are several miles of these roads, which are not plowed in winter, but the homeowners use ski-mobiles to get in and out, thereby providing perfect grooming for cross-country use. The homes themselves have innovative designs and locations and are fun to observe while touring the area.

Whatever kind of skiing you do, there are a pair of hot tubs and a sauna bath to visit afterward in the old lodge building, and following that, a choice of four bars where traditional après-ski conviviality is always underway.

Dining

Besides your own condominium, there are several other good places to eat in Bear Valley, all within an easy stroll from where you live.

The dining room in the old Bear Valley Lodge recently has been renovated and enlarged. It offers full restaurant service for three meals a day, seven days a week, during the ski and summer seasons. Its breakfast menu features omelets and a specialty of mountain trout with eggs, and the lunch menu includes soups, salads, and sandwiches. Any appetite will be satisfied with the steaks, prime ribs, beef en brochette, chicken, and fish offered for dinner.

Downstairs at the Red Dog, another good dining experience is in store for valley visitors. Its small, cozy dining room always has a cheerful fire blazing in a big stone fireplace, which, with the candles on the tables, provides the majority of light. The menu is imaginative, with such unusual items as squid, shark, and Parmesan eggplant along with the more usual veal, pork, beef, and seafood selections. Everything is prepared nicely and served with a choice of soup or a good green salad.

The third dinner house is The Altitude Restaurant, next to the old lodge on the other side of the porte cochere. At the present time, this is the most popular place in the village. It has a lively bar upstairs offering good entertainment and a bustling dining area below, serving good meat and seafood selections and interesting combinations of the two.

Mayfield House

Distance: 205 miles from San Francisco, in Tahoe City
Features: Small, quiet, bed and breakfast inn; centrally located in Tahoe City
Rates: $35 to $55 for two people
Address: 236 Grove Street, Tahoe City, California 95730
Phone: (916) 583-1001

In some areas, pretty little wayside inns abound, but in others, they are a new idea, only just beginning to catch on. Lake Tahoe falls in the latter category, with but one example of this pleasant mode of lodging. The Mayfield House, however, makes a good start. It is advantageously located just a half block off Highway 28, the main street and center of activity, and is within easy walking distance of most shops and restaurants, the public beach, Fanny Bridge, the golf course, a state recreational area, and other cultural attractions. It also serves as a good central location from which to explore the Lake Tahoe area and, in winter, to sample the many ski areas, of which Squaw Valley and Alpine Meadows, two of the best, are but four or five miles away.

Mayfield House is small, with just six guest rooms, but this helps make it quiet and cozy. Room prices include a breakfast of fresh fruit and homemade pastries. For dinner, good nearby restaurants include The Chalet House on the lake, The Pfeifer House for German cooking, and The Tahoe House for Swiss food.

Yosemite Valley

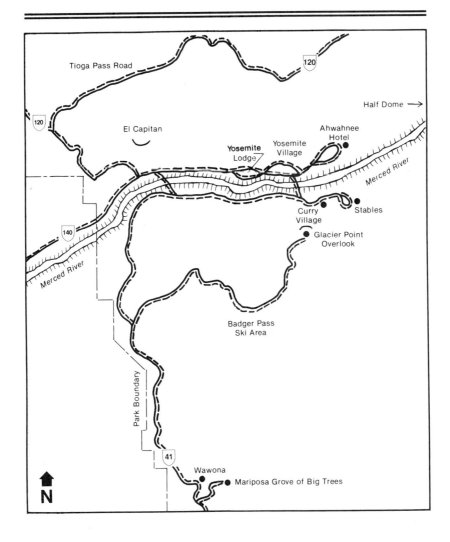

Yosemite Valley

Distances:

From San Francisco—220 miles; allow 5 hours

From Los Angeles—318 miles; allow 7 hours

Features:

Awesome scenery in the "Crown Jewel" of the national park system

Activities:

Hiking, horseback riding, mountain and high-angle rock climbing, nature study, photography, bicycling, river and pool swimming, fishing in summer; downhill and cross-country skiing, outdoor ice skating in winter

Seasons:

Year around; summer season can require reservations well in advance

Rates:

A wide selection of accommodations, with prices ranging from $12.50 for simple tent-cabins to $70 (plus tax) at the hotel; lodge rooms, hotel rooms, and regular cabins available at prices in between

Address:

Reservations Department, Curry Company, Yosemite National Park, California 95389

Phone:

(209) 373-4171

Yosemite's Ahwahnee Hotel

So many spectacular photographs of Yosemite have been published that many people already feel familiar with its famous scenic wonders. What is not so well known is that in this great valley of fabulous rock formations there is also a large, remarkable, year-round resort operated for the benefit of the public.

Yosemite Park is a 1,182-square-mile area that was set aside in order to preserve the wilderness. Most of it is rugged, mountainous country, accessible only to backpackers and people on horseback. The exceptions are a road across the width of the park, open only in summer after the snow has melted, and a small network of accesses in the southwestern corner. It is midway in this corner that a tongue of road leads back into the valley where the resort is located.

The valley was first discovered in 1851 by the Mariposa Battalion of the United States Calvary in hot pursuit of one Chief Tenaya of the Yosemite, or "Grizzly Bear," Indian tribe. Whether the soldiers caught up with the Yosemites, and who won the subsequent battle, is unrecorded, but if the white men were too awed by what they saw to maintain the chase, all who come here will fully understand.

Like the Grand Canyon, Yosemite is one of the great natural phenomena of the West that no American should fail to see. The valley is lined with massive granite cliffs with names such as El Capitan, Cathedral Rocks, Cloud's Rest, Half Dome, and Sentinel Dome. These rise thousands of feet, seemingly straight up, out of the valley floor. And the beautiful, nearly flat land between, through which the wide and clear Merced River begins its long journey to San Francisco Bay and the sea, makes a perfect place for those who love to vacation in the out-of-doors.

But unlike Grand Canyon, into which it is difficult to descend, Yosemite lends itself perfectly to the construction of a resort facility. It first became a national park in 1890, and over the years since then, the awesome, large, and complete complex that now stands was put into place, with much planning and careful development in order to minimize disturbance of the area's natural attributes.

The National Park Service runs the park itself, which has gained the reputation of being the best managed of all our national parks. The service, in turn, contracts with a concessionaire, Yosemite Park & Curry Company, to manage the hotel, lodges, restaurants, and all the amenities tucked among the woods, streams, and meadows of the valley floor. Activities of a dozen sorts are available to suit everyone's whims and energy. There is a ski area within the park, much favored by winter visitors, and a variety of outlying natural attractions, such as groves of two-thousand-year-old giant sequoias; all of these are made accessible by tour buses starting from the valley.

Thanks to its protected status, the park is full of wild animals, including black and brown bear (the grizzlies are gone), deer, porcupines,

Yosemite Lodge, with Bridalveil Fall behind

Sierra marmots, and more than a hundred species of birds. And due to the stark elevation differences, the plant life is varied, with many rare and remarkable kinds of wild flowers to search out and enjoy.

Routes and Distances

From the Bay Area, take U.S. 580 east to Interstate 5 and go south to the Gustine off-ramp, which connects with Route 140. Follow 140 through Merced all the way into Yosemite Park.

From Sacramento and Stockton, take Highway 99 south to Merced and pick up Route 140 there.

The final stretches of Route 140 become increasingly precipitous and scenic, but the roadway is smooth and well maintained, making for an easy drive, although in winter months you need to carry chains and watch for ice as the weather can change rapidly.

A slower route, but more interesting all the way, is to take Highway 16 out of Sacramento to Drytown and then follow Highway 49 for some sixty miles (see the gold country section for information about this interesting trip). Just past Chinese Camp, get on Highway 120, which leads into the park and merges with 140, then follows the Merced River into Yosemite Village.

Accommodations

The Ahwahnee Hotel, Yosemite Lodge, and Curry Village are the places to stay in Yosemite. They are all about a mile and a half apart, tucked away on the valley floor, with the Ahwahnee the oldest and much the grandest choice. Built in 1927, it is a world famous hostelry made from local stone and timber on a scale intended to reflect the magnificence of the natural surroundings. Its 121 rooms are, fittingly, the most elegant quarters available in the park. They are all similar and carry the same nightly rates, except that a few have attached sitting rooms, thus forming suites, and cost an additional sixty dollars per night.

Those who prefer to stay at the lodge or in Curry Village will be well advised to come over to the hotel, at least for dinner, to admire its magnificence. The cavernous lobby has thirty-foot ceilings and back to back walk-in fireplaces with hearths twenty-five feet wide. Off the lobby are library rooms for private gatherings and a solarium with tall windows to accommodate the vertical rise of the view outside. This lobby and its anterooms are the social center for the hotel and are full of heavy lounge furniture, which nevertheless is dwarfed by the rooms themselves. In the evenings, a bar is set up along one side of the lobby for the convenience of guests.

The dining room, which easily can serve several hundred for dinner, is even larger than the lobby, with spectacular pole beam trusses set on fourteen round timber columns, each fashioned from a single tree. In spite of its size, this room is warm and friendly because of the way it is furnished.

Yosemite Lodge is informal, scattered, and quite different in every respect from the hotel. It consists of a number of motellike buildings, cottages, and separate cabins, all grouped around a central core of shops, and containing a total of 474 units of accommodations. The best rooms are called deluxe units and are, in effect, nice motel rooms, with two queen-sized beds and their own little balconies or patios. They are

El Capitan dominates Yosemite Valley

comfortable and are priced at about a third below the cost of accommodations at the Ahwahnee.

For a bit less than that, and next in the order of comfort, are the cottage or standard rooms, which are somewhat more plainly furnished. Then come the individual cabins "with bath and electric heat," for seven dollars a day less than the cottage rooms. Finally, at the low end of the scale and cheaper still are cabins without plumbing, which share central bathing facilities.

Curry Village has more motel rooms, similar to and with the same price range as the lodge's cottage rooms, and also more cabins, with and without baths. The big thing at Curry, however, are the hundreds of tents grouped in clusters like an army bivouac, for people who really want to save money. Each tent is erected on a wooden platform and contains two double-deck steel cots, an electric light, and nothing more. But they are inexpensive. There are six hundred of these various accommodations in the village, widely scattered around a large central pavilion that provides cafeteria dining facilities in summer plus some shops, and an Olympic-sized swimming pool.

To complete the accommodations picture, it should be added that there are eleven campgrounds in the park, mostly out on the Tioga Pass Road. One big one, however, located right in the valley, provides an option for those who do not want the more organized facilities. A surprising number of tents, pitched even in the wintertime, attest to its popularity.

Activities

The valley floor is several miles long and, to permit visitors to get about

Mountaineering school in Yosemite's Curry Village

easily while minimizing automobile traffic, a free shuttle bus operates continually on a big loop conecting the lodge, Yosemite Village, the hotel, and Curry Village. There are also walking and bicycling paths leading everywhere in the valley, with a large supply of bicycles available for rent during spring, summer, and fall at both the lodge and Curry Village. Because the valley is so flat, bicycling is a pleasant way to get oriented and see the sights from different viewpoints. A two-hour guided tour on a bus or, when the weather permits, in open-air trams, also operates year around for those who would rather ride and want to have things explained as they go.

Whether riding, walking, or bicycling, sight-seeing and taking pictures are far and away the main "activities" in which everyone participates. After that, the thousands of visitors divide up according to individual interests. Beyond the valley, for instance, out in the big park itself, are 780 miles of hiking and horseback trails. You can take day hikes, or short rides from the stables, to nearby points, or for longer trips into the backcountry, book out of your accommodations for a few nights and then book back in for the day of your return. The stables where horses are rented and rides arranged are at the Upper Pines camp just past Curry Village. Information about hiking trails is obtained at the Tour Center Desk at the lodge.

For anyone interested in mountaineering, the visit to Yosemite is a splendid opportunity to get started or brush up on old skills. The Yosemite Mountaineering School is located in the Curry Village Pavilion and teaches both beginning and advanced classes during spring and summer. For accomplished climbers, Yosemite has long been the ultimate challenge, attracting the very best talent from all over the world to test their skills against El Capitan and the extraordinarily difficult sheer face of Half Dome.

Other favored summer activities center on the three pools, one at each of the living areas, and on the river, with its numerous beaches and swimming holes. It is popular for rafting and inner-tubing and parts of it, away from the swimming areas, are good for fly fishing. If the river is too tame, there are hundreds of high lakes and tributary streams in the park where rainbows, browns, and eastern brook trout lurk in good numbers.

During winter, Yosemite changes its orientation. Hiking and, of course, photography remain popular, but otherwise activity centers on skiing. The mountaineering school becomes a Nordic ski school, with some ninety miles of marked and groomed cross-country trails. Guided tours and overnight expeditions are arranged by the school and these afford especially fine ways to see the scenery.

Downhill skiing takes place at Badger Pass, which is reached by a twenty-three-mile drive on the Glacier Point Road. Free shuttle buses make this trip from the valley all winter. Badger, with three chairs and two T-bars, was California's first established ski area. Today, it is relatively small compared with some of the newer developments, but it can handle up to three thousand people on busy weekends. It is considered a family-oriented ski area, with many enjoyable runs but none that are really difficult. Classes and instructions are available for all levels of ability. Skiers should inquire about the special packages that are designed to encourage midweek use of the facilities and include lodging, lift tickets, and ski school instruction at a single, reduced price.

In addition to skiing, the other major winter sport at Yosemite is outdoor ice skating on the large, well-kept rink at Curry Village. The skating season usually extends from mid-November through mid-March, with rental equipment available at the mountaineering school.

Dining

We suggested earlier the desirability of having dinner one night at the Ahwahnee Hotel, even though you may stay at the lodge or at Curry Village. The experience both of seeing the hotel and having an elegant meal in a beautiful room are very much worthwhile, though somewhat expensive, and the shuttle will take you there and bring you back. A word to the wise: during the winter there sometimes are informal ski buffets on Thursday nights; otherwise, it is customary for men to wear ties and jackets in the hotel dining room. Advance reservations are almost always a necessity for dinner.

The Curry Village cafeteria is quite the opposite: completely casual in all respects. It is open for business only in spring and summer, so guests take the shuttle to the lodge for their meals in winter.

Curry Village's outdoor ice skating rink in Yosemite Valley

At the lodge is a huge cafeteria, a bar, and two restaurants, all housed along with some shops in a large building across a terrace from the offices and registration area. The cafeteria, especially in winter when people are coming back from Badger Pass, resembles a typical ski lodge, furnished for utilitarian efficiency and very busy. The restaurants offer more style and comfort. The first of these is the Four Seasons, which offers a general menu, including seafood. The other is the Mountain Room restaurant, which is a broiler with appropriately specialized fare. Neither of these takes reservations, but they will put you on a waiting list in order of arrival and announce on the public address system when your table is ready. People wait in the Mountain Room Bar, situated between the two restaurants, or, in nice weather, on the terrace outside.

One other option for eating at Yosemite is The Deli, which is located in Yosemite Village in a loft above a delicatessen-grocery. The Deli specializes in chili and fast foods and has a bar and a big central fireplace around which people like to gather after a day outdoors.

Checklist

House
- House key
- Babysitter and dog-sitter arranged
- Doors and windows locked
- Furnace turned down
- Water and electric lights turned off
- Neighbor to take in mail and newspapers arranged

Packing
- Casual clothes
- Dinner clothes
- Walking shoes
- Bathing suits and robes
- Toilet articles

Personal
- Money and checkbook
- Glasses and sunglasses
- Reservation confirmations
- Camera and film

Sports Equipment
- Binoculars
- Bicycles
- Tennis gear
- Golf gear
- Fishing tackle
- Clamming equipment
- Rain gear
- Skiing gear
- Rucksack

Refreshments
- Thermos of coffee
- Breakfast ingredients
- Beverages
- Snacks

Auto
- Extra set of car keys
- Chains (in winter)
- Full gas tank

Other Books from Pacific Search Press

The Apple Cookbook by Kyle D. Fulwiler
Asparagus: The Sparrowgrass Cookbook by Autumn Stanley
The Berry Cookbook by Kyle D. Fulwiler
The Birdhouse Book: Building Houses, Feeders, and Baths by Don McNeil
Bone Appétit! Natural Foods for Pets by Frances Sheridan Goulart
Border Boating: Twelve Cruises through the San Juan and Gulf Islands by
    Phyllis and Bill Bultmann
Butterflies Afield in the Pacific Northwest by William Neill/Douglas
    Hepburn, photography
The Carrot Cookbook by Ann Saling
Cascade Companion by Susan Schwartz/Bob and Ira Spring, photography
Common Seaweeds of the Pacific Coast by J. Robert Waaland
The Complete Guide to Organic Gardening West of the Cascades by Steve
    Solomon
The Crawfish Cookbook by Norma S. Upson
Cross-Country Downhill and Other Nordic Mountain Skiing Techniques
    (2d Ed. Revised & Enlarged) by Steve Barnett
*Cruising the Columbia and Snake Rivers: Eleven Cruises in the Inland
    Waterway* by Sharlene P. Nelson and Joan LeMieux
The Dogfish Cookbook by Russ Mohney
The Eggplant Cookbook by Norma S. Upson
Fire and Ice: The Cascade Volcanoes (Revised Ed.) by Stephen L. Harris
The Getaway Guide: Short Vacations in the Pacific Northwest by Marni
    and Jake Rankin
The Getaway Guide II: More Short Vacations in the Pacific Northwest
    by Marni and Jake Rankin
The Green Tomato Cookbook by Paula Simmons
The Guide to Successful Tapestry Weaving by Nancy Harvey
The Handspinner's Guide to Selling by Paula Simmons
The House Next Door: Seattle's Neighborhood Architecture by Lila
    Gault/Mary Randlett, photography
Little Mammals of the Pacific Northwest by Ellen B. Kritzman
Living Shores of the Pacific Northwest by Lynwood Smith/Bernard Nist,
    photography
Make It and Take It: Homemade Gear for Camp and Trail by Russ Mohney
Marine Mammals of Eastern North Pacific and Arctic Waters edited by
    Delphine Haley
Messages from the Shore by Victor B. Scheffer
Minnie Rose Lovgreen's Recipe for Raising Chickens by Minnie Rose
    Lovgreen
Mushrooms 'n Bean Sprouts: A First Step for Would-be Vegetarians by
    Norma M. MacRae, R.D.

My Secret Cookbook by Paula Simmons
The Natural Fast Food Cookbook by Gail L. Worstman
The Northwest Adventure Guide by Pacific Search Press
Rhubarb Renaissance: A Cookbook by Ann Saling
The Salmon Cookbook by Jerry Dennon
Seattle Photography by David Barnes
Sleek & Savage: North America's Weasel Family by Delphine Haley
Spinning and Weaving with Wool by Paula Simmons
Starchild & Holahan's Seafood Cookbook by Adam Starchild and James
    Holahan
They Tried to Cut It All by Edwin Van Syckle
Two Crows Came by Jonni Dolan
The Whole Grain Bake Book by Gail L. Worstman
Wild Mushroom Recipes by Puget Sound Mycological Society
Wild Shrubs: Finding and Growing Your Own by Joy Spurr
The Zucchini Cookbook by Paula Simmons